ANTITRUST LAWS

The Case of Facebook v FTC

TOMORROW'S WORLD ORDER'S PERSPECTIVE

By

David Gomadza

TOMORROW'S WORLD ORDER'S PERSPECTIVE

Antitrust Laws
The Case of Facebook v FTC

TOMORROW'S WORLD ORDER'S PERSPECTIVE

TOMORROW'S WORLD ORDER'S PERSPECTIVE

DEDICATION

Tomorrow's World Order

We are a global phenomenon to lead humanity out of the defensive stages towards networking and cooperation as nature intended. We strongly believe that humankind has failed. The current system has crashed and now not fit for purpose and we are here to lead humanity out of the defensive stages simply because for the past seventy years global issues have worsened with a global debt of more than $244 trillion, with all recent financial crises, poverty, unemployment, climatic change, wars, and political instability and all issues to do with inadequate global finances. We strongly believe that the current system has crashed and as such only a new system will ultimately solve today's global problems, hence the rise of Tomorrow's World Order. We are here to guide humankind and act as overseers to lay the correct path for humanity to take to solve all current and future global problems. For the past 2000 years, humankind has been stuck in the defensive stages where defense plays a key role in whatever humanity does. Mainly out of fear of the unknown or as a means of getting the resources he cannot afford cheaply. Where $1.7 trillion is plowed yearly globally into defense, making weapons, and relying on weapons and defense as the drivers of the economy. This has meant humanity opting for the cheaper ways of doing things yet the most destructive ones; killing innocent women and children in the process, making cheaper weapons, and using these to get the most expensive resources he cannot afford. *Enacting laws: be it antitrust laws, etc. to get the resources he needs cheaply and unfairly mainly from hard-working people. Added.* We strongly think this is not only barbaric but shows that humankind has failed to think outside of the box. We as a people are running below our potential. Mankind's current system is very wasteful, with $trillion globally plowed into weapons manufacturing and the military at the expense of other areas. Humanity is changing nevertheless at a slow pace and everyone has now realized that we all ought to be networking and cooperating and working towards becoming friends for global peace's sake. Yet humankind still manufactures weapons and invests heavily in the military when the world is moving toward global peace. Who are we going to use the weapons on, especially when sworn enemies like the USA and North Korea are now on talking terms? We know the current system crashed years ago with the last financial crisis, yet humanity has stuck to this system that is not fit for purpose. We have come up with a global solution to all global problems, and our method will emancipate all nations and create wealth levels never witnessed before. Our system is the only answer to global problems, and we are going to take humankind to the next stage of development creating wealth never witnessed before.

TOMORROW'S WORLD ORDER'S PERSPECTIVE

Table of Contents

EXECUTIVE SUMMARY OF NOTEWORTHY POINTS.   1

I.   1

SWOT ANALYSIS   1

SELF DEFENSE   1

TRUSTS   2

THE RISE OF TOMORROW'S WORLD ORDER.   2

RULE OF REASON.   2

A DETAILED ANALYSIS OF FACEBOOK'S OPPORTUNITIES TO CLARIFY THE MISTAKE BY THE FTC.   10

MISCONCEPTIONS IN WHAT CONSTITUTES A THREAT TO FACEBOOK. TO US AS TOMORROW'S WORLD ORDER WHATSAPP AND INSTAGRAM ARE OPPORTUNITIES TO FACEBOOK.   12

MATCHING AND CONVERTING AS A STRATEGY RATHER THAN COMPETING AS SUGGESTED BY THE FTC AND THEIR ANTITRUST LAWS BY FACEBOOK IN ACQUIRING WHATSAPP AND INSTAGRAM.   12

WHATSAPP AND INSTAGRAM AS FACEBOOK'S OPPORTUNITIES RATHER THAN ITS THREATS.   15

INDIRECT KILLING OF COMPETITION BY FACEBOOK THROUGH OFFERING HUGE SUMS TO NEW START UPS. BUT HOW CAN THAT BE ANTICOMPETITIVE BEHAVIOR IN THE MEANING OF THE ANTITRUST LAWS.   19

CORPORATIONS INVOLVED IN THE SECRET HACKING TOO AS ACCOMPLICES.   26

ANTITRUST FINES AS FEES FOR USING ILLEGAL TECHNOLOGY AND VIOLATING GOVERNMENTS COPYRIGHTS. GOVERNMENTS AS SNOOPING SPICES.   27

GOVERNMENT SNOOPING AND ACTING AS SPIES. CONVERTING CITIZEN'S THOUGHTS TO TEXT TO HELP CORPORATIONS IN ITS ANALYSIS OF DATA.   30

TOMORROW'S WORLD ORDER'S PERSPECTIVE

THE POSSIBLE ALTERNATIVE TO FACEBOOK IS DIGIBOOK MY OWN INVENTION. 31

ABILITY TO INVENT SOMETHING WHERE NO ONE CAN FIND AN ALTERNATIVE DOES NOT AMOUNT TO HARM TO COMPETITION. 34

THE TRICKERY, DEVIOUS AND MANIPULATING ACTS OF THE FTC. 36

FINES OR FEES? 37

TALK OF HARM TO COMPETITION IS FLAWED. 38

ROLE OF ECONOMIES OF SCALE. 39

THE INTERSTATE'S PERSONAL SURVIVAL STRATEGY RATHER THAN CALLS TO INCREASE COMPETITION. 40

A VICIOUS CYCLE OF ABUSE. 42

A GRANT OF A RELIEF THAT IS USED TO FURTHER ABUSE THE VICTIMS IS NO RELIEF AT ALL. 45

WHERE THE GOVERNMENT DOES THE SAME TO ITS CITIZENS, IT HAS NO RECOURSE TO THE ARGUMENT OF A RELIEF. 45

TALKING OF OUTDATED LAWS. 45

THE BILLION DOLLAR CONGRESS. 47

REWARDING THE INABILITY TO DEAL WITH ECONOMIC PRESSURES. 48

THE LAWSUIT IS THERE ONLY TO CREATE A BILLION-DOLLAR FTC AND ITS INTERSTATE SOMETHING WE CAN ONLY ASSOCIATE WITH MAGIC AND WISHFUL THINKING. 50

II. 52

GENERAL VIEWS AT THE TIME. 52

CONDITIONS IN 1890 JUST BEFORE THE ENACTMENT OF THE SHERMAN ACT. 52

DIRECT AND HIDDEN MOTIVES BEHIND THE SHERMAN ACT. 52

THE PROBLEM AT HAND. 53

TOMORROW'S WORLD ORDER'S PERSPECTIVE

MISUNDERSTANDINGS OF THE IMPORTANT ROLE OF ECONOMIES OF SCALE. 54

VICIOUS CYCLE VERSUS VIRTUOUS CYCLE. 54

LOW-QUALITY PRODUCTS AND SERVICES. 55

COMPLEX PROCEDURES. 56

REGULATORY BURDEN AS AN OBSTACLE AND THE CURRENT SYSTEM. 56

LACK OF MARKET FORCES. 56

III. 58

OUR VIEW OF THE SITUATION AND THE ROAD TO THE VIRTUOUS CYCLE. 58

FACILITATION. 59

LAWS AGAINST THE GOVERNMENT, THE INTERSTATE, AND THE FEDERAL TRADE COMMISSION, ETC. 61

THE SHIFT IN EMPHASIS FROM THE REGULATORY BURDEN TO FACILITATION THEN TO A NEW ADVANCED STAGE OF DEVELOPMENT WHERE THERE ARE TANGIBLE BENEFITS. 62

IV. 63

THE RIGHT OF CORPORATIONS TO USE THE SWOT ANALYSIS. 63

ANTICOMPETITIVE ALLEGATIONS FLAWED FROM OUTSET. AS SMALL COMPANIES WERE CREATED TO BE SOLD AT A PROFIT TO FACEBOOK ANYWHERE. 64

FREEDOM OF ACTIONS. 65

FIRST, YOU MUST UNDERSTAND THAT THE WHOLE SYSTEM IS BASED ON THE PYRAMID SYSTEM. 66

PYRAMID SCHEMES. 66

V. 69

OUR DIAMOND-SHAPED SYSTEM VERSUS THE CURRENT SYSTEM OF THE

TOMORROW'S WORLD ORDER'S PERSPECTIVE

PYRAMID.   69

CURRENT PYRAMID SYSTEM AND ITS CHECKS TO KEEP IT IN CONTROL
AND PLACE.   70

OUR SYSTEM THE DIAMOND SHAPE VERSUS THE CURRENT PYRAMID.73

VI.   75

THE ONLY WAY FORWARD. NO CHECKS AND CONTROLS.   75

TOMORROW'S WORLD ORDER AS THE ANSWER TO FACEBOOK AND
OTHER COMPANIES' GROWTH AND THREATS.   77

VII.   80

GOVERNMENTS AS THE MASTER MINDERS AND VEHICLES OF MODERN-
DAY SECRET SLAVERY AND OPPRESSION OF THEIR PEOPLE. THEY HAVE
BECOME ANTI MANKIND.   80

THE ISSUE OF ROLLBACK IS COUNTERPRODUCTIVE. THE ISSUE OF THE
VICIOUS CYCLE.   82

VIII.   85

STEALING AND COPYRIGHT VIOLATIONS BY THE GOVERNMENTS AND
THE INTERSTATE AND THE FEDERALS AS A FACTOR AGAINST THE
ANTITRUST LAWS.   85

DOUBLE STANDARDS.   87

IX.   88

THE POLITICAL ASPECTS OF THESE TRUSTS AND CORPORATIONS.   88

SELF-CONTRADICTIONS.   89

TIME FOR CORPORATIONS AND TRUST TO TAKE A LEADING ROLE.   89

CASE STUDY   89

FACEBOOK VERSUS THE US ATTORNEY. ANTITRUST LAWSUIT.   89

X.   93

RECOMMENDATIONS AND THE WAY FORWARD.   93

TOMORROW'S WORLD ORDER'S PERSPECTIVE

FACILITATION RATHER THAN A REGULATORY BURDEN.　　94

NEED TO ACKNOWLEDGE THE INADEQUACIES OF THE CURRENT SYSTEM
IN DEALING WITH THE EVER-GROWING CORPORATIONS.　　95

ABOUT DAVID GOMADZA　　97

ACKNOWLEDGMENTS

A big thanks to Tomorrow's World Order.

TOMORROW'S WORLD ORDER'S PERSPECTIVE

EXECUTIVE SUMMARY OF NOTEWORTHY POINTS.
Antitrust Laws
The Case of Facebook v FTC

TOMORROW'S WORLD ORDER'S PERSPECTIVE

I.

SWOT ANALYSIS

It is a strategic planning technique used to help a person or organization identify strengths, weaknesses, opportunities, and threats related to business competition or project planning.
Wikipedia.

SELF DEFENSE

 (self-defense in some varieties of English) is a countermeasure that involves defending the health and well-being of oneself from harm.[1] The use of the right of self-defense as a legal justification for the use of force in times of danger is available in many jurisdictions. Wikipedia.

Since corporations are legal entities, it is open to me to argue that Facebook can use the right to self-defense concerning its handling of the crisis posed by the rise of smartphones that triggered the need for a new system or change as this new technological development rendered their computer-based photo and messaging system near obsolete. Whatever they did, cannot fall into anticompetitive behavior but under a survival strategy. Facebook can argue that it acted in the way it did, namely; buying WhatsApp and Instagram, not as a competitive strategy to put others out of business. See below in detail. But as a Crisis Management strategy to defend itself from the threats of new technology and not the rivalry of smaller companies mentioned above to remain in business. Facebook might have used its money to buy these not to keep all out even though emails might say exactly that but to stay in business. After all, the two companies might have been better off after all. They had the future, but because Facebook is not a bully as the antitrust lawsuit is implying.

TOMORROW'S WORLD ORDER'S PERSPECTIVE

They paid even a better price for the two companies because if that were not the case, the owners could have refused to sell. They got a better deal as compared to the value of their companies. In most cases, Facebook is the trigger for the formation of the companies in the first place. Therefore, must be credited with the formations of the companies in the first place and not their exit or fall. Read below.

TRUSTS

These are groups of businesses that combine their resources and come together forming a monopoly in the process which will end up deciding the prices in a market.

THE RISE OF TOMORROW'S WORLD ORDER.

It is not surprising that the world's powerful and richest entities are corporations rather than governments. Most have a huge market share which they use to get political influence. Then use this political influence to further maintain and increase their market share. As the market share continues to grow, hence the political influence until a time when even the current law establishment will not be able to handle them. That signals the need for a new legal and political framework to match and deal with these ever-growing corporations and trusts. This triggered the rise of Tomorrow's World Order.

RULE OF REASON.

Not all actions by big companies can be said to harm the consumers. Apart from the obvious illegal acts like fixing the price. Some actions must be analyzed in relation to their benefits to the consumer if they do not fall in the restraint of trade category. Meaning the courts cannot outright judge just by looking at the anti-competitive nature of the business but also must apply the rule of reason to assess the benefits to the consumer or public good.

1. First and foremost, I want to argue that what one uses and does in Crisis Management cannot be regarded as anticompetitive behavior. To some extent, it is flawed to

use antitrust laws for acts or actions done when a business was heading for disaster. That can amount to a survival technique bearing in mind that no actions can justify illegality. The corporation here Facebook needs to prove that it was facing a threat that could have seen them ceasing functioning. The questions to answer are; Was Facebook in a position to either do or die? Did it act within the law? If for example was Facebook going to go out of business due to the 'unforeseeable and of big magnitude threats' in the form of the rise of smartphones, etc. at the very moment in time? If yes, then this can fall under a Crisis management task to stay in business. This is like people who use the self-defense argument in murder cases as they acted to preserve their own life? Mind you, a business is a legal entity with its rights that it can sue and be sued. As such, it can be argued in my view. Those acts such as the acquisition of WhatsApp and Instagram by Facebook were self-defense acts. Acts done to stay in business. Acts not to deal with threats but acts to deal with the Opportunities [see SWOT analysis below] of Facebook as a business. All this meaning the antitrust laws have no bearing and are flawed. The acts to fall under crisis management must be *a disruptive and unexpected event that threatens to harm the organization or its stakeholders. Wikipedia.*

2. Threats to Facebook were the rise of smartphones and their photo messaging features. This was the threat. Since there is a threat, that means the old system of doing things has changed or must change. The business either changes or ceases to exist. This herald the need for change. It is now a survival strategy. Whatever the corporation or its CEO does here is not something to do with competition as the way the Antitrust laws were enacted to deal with. These laws are misinterpreted and applied everywhere where the FTC, the

Interstates, and the Department of Justice think it is lucrative to extract some easy quick dosh.

3. Different environments. High digital technological environment versus the activities the Sherman Act was enacted to deal with such as the rise of oil refinery industries such as in the Standard Oil case. The technological industry is different, and I think caution must be exercised in dealing with these.

4. The need for a complete change as a disruptive and unexpected event versus the competition and anticompetitive behavior as in oil refinery industries.

5. Facebook faced an existence-threatening event with the rise of smartphones. That means that Facebook, unless if it changed then it will cease to exist. That means a system change was needed. Note the difference. It is not a competitive strategy or anti-competition one to grow bigger here. This is a technological digital market. It is about survival. Such as in self-defense cases. Acts like acquiring WhatsApp and Instagram are beyond the antitrust laws.

6. I think it will be beneficial here to look at the difference between Crisis Management and Risk Management and see how they relate to the Antitrust Laws and the case at hand the Facebook versus FTC.

7. Antitrust laws were enacted to deal with acts done in Risk Management and not ones in Crisis Management. Anticompetitive acts have everything to do with risk management. The competitive behavior is associated more with risk management than with crisis management. In risk management companies assess and analyze their potential threats and deal with these. They employ all the tactics Facebook is being accused of using. This is planning for potential future threats. Note here the magic word is potential. Whereas in crisis management the threat is present.

8. Please note the time element here which is important to determine whether an act is a risk management planning and therefore an anticompetitive act or a crisis planning act, therefore a survival act that falls into self-defense.

9. There is time to plan for potential threats. Where the company can plan all the anticompetitive tactics. This is not the case in crisis management, as time can be a factor. Okay, they might take longer to buy WhatsApp or Instagram, but it is in relation to the time needed to change the system as the past system becomes obsolete. In the case of Facebook, technological development in the rise of smartphones herald the end of the computer-based system of Facebook. This has nothing to do with competition, the very type of competition referred to by the Antitrust Laws. Facebook is not acquiring WhatsApp and Instagram as a tactic to kill the competition because they are not in the same category. But is dealing with a crisis that requires immediate action even though this might take months to do. It is not about assessing and mitigating future potential threats, but the presence of the threat that triggered the merger or acquisition.

10. Facebook's purchase of WhatsApp and Instagram cannot be referred to as competition in the meaning of the antitrust laws. In that, we are talking about two different categories of technological advancement. Facebook is the weak side as they are using obsolete systems or technologies and are on the verge of going out of business at the time in question. Whereas WhatsApp and Instagram are the new advanced technologies making lucrative deals to Facebook. So, the talk of anti-competitive allegations is flawed. It is different from the Standard Oil case where standard oil is powerful here, buying out all and creating barriers to competition. Facebook is pulling the rope off the quicksand. It is not trying to drag the smaller companies into quicksand.

11. An especially serious point critical to this case here is that it is not Facebook in control and therefore it cannot be a bully enough to push others out. Picture a huge hungry snake swallowing all the smaller snakes just because it can and is hungry. Seen that? Okay, now picture a huge snake being swallowed by quicksand. Seen that. Now picture two smaller snakes holding the huge snake's head and pulling it hard out of the quicksand. Seen that. Now breathe. Relax and tell me if the antitrust laws apply in this case? Honestly, if you stand for justice not. The rise of smartphones created a quicksand that it was only a matter of time before it took Facebook. The small snakes saw it even before Facebook anticipated this. As a business model then created a business with Facebook in mind so that they sell the business to Facebook when the time comes. They are heroes of Facebook, and behind the scenes idolize Facebook. But this is a business model and is not to please anyone. What matters is a lucrative deal helping Facebook and making a kill too. The talk of killing competition is a misconception of how digital technology works. Applying antitrust laws casually here is a miscarriage of justice. If Facebook is guilty of anything, it might have to do with privacy or invasion or misuse of data. But something they have already dealt with. Most of the smaller competition the FTC talks about are startup businesses created to solve big giant's technological problems in the future at a lucrative deal. They created the companies so that Facebook ends up buying them. Facebook is their end goal, not as the FTC wants to put it that they are there to grow as big as Facebook. Most anticipate the downfall of such a big giant then produce solutions as a business model because they know Facebook will need their ideas and will buy at a lucrative deal because it is something essential to their

survival. So, they are there waiting for the crisis to happen and come forward and make a deal.

12. Surely the rise of smartphones can fit that definition. That is unexpected and the rise of smartphone phones brought a challenge and threat to Facebook's existence. Even though in Facebook's emails the CEO referred to WhatsApp and Instagram as threats, these were their opportunities as in SWOT analysis. See below.

13. Corporations and Trusts follow the company's laws that are fair and anti-discriminatory. They forbid all kinds of illegalities and place a huge burden on corporations to be fair and act accordingly. To have a duty of care to the consumers, etc.

14. Corporations and Trusts use methods taught and approved at the university level to be used for them to become, 'a cut above the rest'. To gain a competitive edge. Only a competitive edge will dictate the failure or success of a business. Get a competitive edge, then your market share increases as well. That means huge profits, which unfortunately also dictates the exit of many players. What the FTC and the government agencies are calling acts of killing the competition. This is a natural and mandatory criterion or path to success. But it is not over yet even after achieving this as they must grow to take advantage of economies of scale.

15. But to do that, they must grow bigger. To grow bigger they must merge or increase assets like capital and building to increase production. This is the only way they will gain and use economies of scale to supply high-quality products at lower prices. To achieve that, they must use a technique that is popular in business circles. One that uses a method that is often highlighted as a means of analyzing the business' position to ascertain the competitiveness of a business and determine the strategy to take. The SWOT

TOMORROW'S WORLD ORDER'S PERSPECTIVE

analysis. Meaning an abbreviation of the Strength of the company, then the analysis of its Weakness. Then of its Opportunities and lastly of its Threats. You must understand that this is a university taught tool to urge forward competitively. The idea behind this is to outsmart your opponents to get that prize of being the number one and only one. This is the only goal of all businesses. That will mean a raised market share. That means huge profits in return. That means huge incentives to invest. That means realizing the economies of scale which in turn means reduced costs greatly. As volume increases in turn means increases in efficiency as well. This means selling many products at lower prices. That means the best prices to the consumers. In the case of Facebook that can mean reduced advertising space but most importantly of high quality. Mergers have meant Facebook achieving economies of scale. They can sell space to many people and can afford to reduce prices and the adverts are of the highest quality in terms of speed and exposure as well as they can advertise to many people on their platforms, etc. All this can be achieved through the SWOT analysis. It is mandatory to ACT on the identified entity, be it a threat and or a Weakness etc. But I will elaborate further here. A business's existence is not dependent on itself alone. The biggest menace to a business's existence is its threats. Threats can mean fewer profits. Threats are competitors here. Other businesses. Especially the new startups. These can eat away your market share and cut your profit margin, etc. So, businesses here target threats as a survival technique. But all the strategies they employ to neutralize the threat are tactics taught at the university and most within the company laws. Meaning lawful in the company law which gives, the businesses their existence. The threats here are the ones that give rise to the antitrust laws. So, the FTC looks at the threats to a company like Facebook and analyzes or investigates what Facebook has done to deal with the threat to discover the anticompetitive acts. This applies to most business models. But I want to argue here that in the technological and digital environment this analysis is flawed. Ok, if it was Standard oil's dealings with its threats as in other small oil companies then the FTC might be right to cry foul play. As anti-competitive laws would have been breached. I will explain why the analysis in the digital technology industry is flawed.

16. Again, I will visit the SWOT analysis technique and use it to show why the FTC got everything wrong. In the SWOT analysis technique; WhatsApp and Instagram are not threats to Facebook. Yes, small oil companies are threats to Standard oil. But come on. To Facebook, these companies are not their threats, as in the SWOT analysis. They fall under the OPPORTUNITIES to Facebook. So outright the FTC got it wrong to say Facebook uses anticompetitive tactics to its 'Opportunities'. Come on people. Read between the lines. Facebook will never use anticompetitive tactics to its OPPORTUNITIES. Facebook will woo its opportunities. I will argue here that if the FTC wants to accuse Facebook of some wrongdoing, they must say that Facebook sweet-talked too much of its Opportunities and make the allegations and take them to court. That I will accept. You will never use dirty on your Opportunities. How can you woo a woman with threats? Absurd. The law needs to be understood.

17. I know the FTC might say we have the CEO of Facebook in his own words referring to the small companies; WhatsApp and Instagram as their threats. We have this in print as well. To hell with that. People boast of power in all kinds of ways. The CEO might want to feel dominant and powerful. He might refer to an Opportunity as a threat because he did not know that when Instagram and WhatsApp were created,

they had him at the center of the business drawing plan. Their business models. So, your honor, ladies, and gentlemen if you want to accuse the CEO of dirty tactics then I agree with you. For his crime, here is to think of his protégés as threats. These people have modeled on him, but little did he know. They might have thought that if we play cool with him, idolize him, etc., then they are not going to get as much as they might get when they sell to him as stiff competitors. So, to get the most, they played as ruthless rivals. But just to get in and get out as they seal that lucrative deal before they start another company to sell to another tech giant. You must understand the business world. Sometimes you might pretend to do everything to win, even fight the very person you build your business for. So, you get that lucrative deal. So, the CEO might have been in the dark thinking his opportunities are his threats. So, in that light basing the evidence on the emails is flawed and cannot be allowed.

18. In the heat of the moment.

The emails can only be referred to as things said and done in the heat of the moment. Secondly, the time and age and the achievements of the CEO at the time of the emails might have played a significant role. As a young man who has achieved what others might never have achieved before. He might have said that even though he knew that the companies were formulated to be sold to him.

19. A DETAILED ANALYSIS OF FACEBOOK'S OPPORTUNITIES TO CLARIFY THE MISTAKE BY THE FTC.

I argued above that the SWOT analysis is a business tool used by most companies directly or indirectly to assess the business's competitive position.

The antitrust laws are concerned with the ways the business reacts and does to the competition. It is also fair to look at how the business assesses its competitive advantage.

TOMORROW'S WORLD ORDER'S PERSPECTIVE

SWOT analysis (or **SWOT matrix**) is a <u>strategic planning</u> technique used to help a person or organization identify strengths, weaknesses, opportunities, and threats related to <u>business</u> competition... Wikipedia.
SWOT assumes that strengths and weaknesses are frequently internal, while opportunities and threats are more commonly external.[2] The name is an acronym for the four parameters the technique examines:
- *Strengths*: characteristics of the business or project that give it an advantage over others.
- *Weaknesses*: characteristics that place the business or project at a disadvantage relative to others.
- *Opportunities*: elements in the environment that the business or project could exploit to its advantage.
- *Threats*: elements in the environment that could cause trouble for the business or project.

Wikipedia [1]

20. Facebook deduced the view of WhatsApp and Instagram that dictates the tactics towards these as Threats or Opportunities.

I want to argue that the category in which Instagram and WhatsApp fall into in Facebook's analysis of its competitive advantage, through the SWOT analysis, points to how Facebook viewed them and the way they reacted to them. That determined also the way they dealt with them. Put aside for a moment the view that even the CEO himself viewed these namely WhatsApp and Instagram as his threats in his correspondence. We can deduce the way he dealt with these and the exact way they were viewed by Facebook subconsciously.

21. To me, I believe that in Facebook's view; Instagram, and WhatsApp are Opportunities rather than Threats. That follows also that if they are Opportunities, then they are not competitive entities to Facebook. So, the antitrust laws which are about competition do not apply here to Instagram and WhatsApp as these are Facebook's Opportunities. In which case, Facebook has a right or I ought to give them the right to sue these, namely; the FTC and the Department of Justice for invasion and intrusion in the affairs that do not concern them.

TOMORROW'S WORLD ORDER'S PERSPECTIVE

The antitrust laws do not apply to opportunities of a company because they woo the Opportunities like wooing a woman, so the talk about dirty anticompetitive tactics is flawed.
These are my arguments.

i.   In the SWOT analysis, Strengths and Opportunities are helpful to Facebook. While the Weakness and threats are harmful.

ii.   To add to that is the fact that Strengths and Weaknesses are internal to the organization. While the Opportunities and Threats are external to Facebook.

iii.   Three elements are common to a crisis: (a) a threat to the organization, (b) the element of surprise, and (c) a short decision time. Wikipedia [2.]

22. MISCONCEPTIONS IN WHAT CONSTITUTES A THREAT TO FACEBOOK. TO US AS TOMORROW'S WORLD ORDER WHATSAPP AND INSTAGRAM ARE OPPORTUNITIES TO FACEBOOK.

23. I want to point out here that the threats to Facebook were not Instagram and WhatsApp as the FTC and the Department of Justice and their interstates want to make it look. A threat to Facebook was not the above, but the rise of smartphones with instant photo messaging tools. This was a threat to Facebook. Crisis Management then identified an Opportunity to solve this as the acquisition of WhatsApp and Instagram. This has significant implications in that it also dictates the method employed by Facebook to deal with these. This will answer the antitrust allegations as well. Whether its acts were anti-competitive or not or whether the antitrust apply at all here.

24. MATCHING AND CONVERTING AS A STRATEGY RATHER THAN COMPETING AS SUGGESTED BY THE FTC AND THEIR ANTITRUST LAWS BY FACEBOOK IN ACQUIRING WHATSAPP AND INSTAGRAM.

First, I must look at the definition of antitrust laws.

25. **Antitrust laws** are statutes developed by governments to protect consumers from predatory business practices and ensure fair competition. Investopedia. In the United States, antitrust law is a collection of federal and state government laws that regulate the conduct and organization of business corporations and are generally intended to promote competition for the benefit of consumers. Wikipedia.

26. The underlying phrases here are to "ensure fair competition" and to "promote competition".

27. You must understand that technology change heralds the need for system change. As I have pointed out below, facing is not competing or employing competitive tactics in its acquisition dealings but matching and converting as a survival strategy. Standard oil was competing with smaller companies and engaging in predatory acts because it was the market leader. They were all trading the same products. Facebook was nearly ceasing to operate as their technology had been found to be out of date and in touch with the new taste of the people. So, it adopted a Match and Convert strategy to stay in business. It was the loser and not the market dominator. This was a new technology. It had to match first and then convert its own and the acquired to current standards.

28. So far in this analysis, Facebook then knew there was a crisis looming. So, it identified the crisis. The rise in new technology in smartphones and their photo applications. Secondly, Facebook identified the strategy to take as an explorer rather than as a bully, unlike the way the FTC wants to portray. It now knew what needed to be done. It is not competing because the others are in a league of their own. First, they must match the others and use the

same technology, but to do so requires them to deal with threats and opportunities. Initially, they might have viewed WhatsApp and Instagram as threats. So, they waited and observed. Weeks and months go by and then they realized that these companies are not going anywhere. They are waiting for a lucrative offer from them. Okay, they are aggressively making it look like they are rivals. Facebook is the snake in the quicksand sinking. These two are to help. They are Opportunities for Facebook to turn things around.

29. The need to match rather than compete makes Facebook regard these as positive welcome opportunities.

30. Since Facebook has an inferior product to them, they can only position themselves alongside and make them see the importance of Facebook as a tech giant with a lot of financial resources to solve any problems of these two companies; WhatsApp and Instagram. So, they make themselves attractive to them. If they were not, surely WhatsApp and Instagram would not have sold to them. The tactics are to attract. Rules of attraction do not include competitive behavior, never mind dirty tactics. In most cases, the small companies are like orphans waiting just to be adopted. If Facebook does not see the need to, that breaks them and heralds their exit. So here Facebook indirectly is doing good to these. Buying them as the means that fulfill the end. Without Facebook, they would not have been formed. If Facebook had not bought them, they would have failed to realize their goal.

31. FACEBOOK AS A FACILITATOR OF COMPETITION AND THE GROWTH OF THESE SMALL COMPANIES PROVIDING VALUE FOR THE CUSTOMER.

32. All other companies are being created to fill a gap in technology when needed at a lucrative price. They have the ideas and know exactly what Facebook will need and therefore provide that as a business model to later sell to

Facebook. So, Facebook is not killing competition but triggering competition indirectly. Most of the small companies would rather sell to Facebook than compete with it. Otherwise, they would not have sold.

33. Now the reason for dealing with the threats and opportunities is to show you the methods used for each and how they relate or not relate to antitrust laws.

34. Okay, everything is to do with getting a competitive advantage to become the market leader. A company or corporation can never use predatory tactics to its Opportunities.

35. WHATSAPP AND INSTAGRAM AS FACEBOOK'S OPPORTUNITIES RATHER THAN ITS THREATS.

36. That brings me to the big point I want to make. Facebook's dealings with WhatsApp and Instagram were to see them as positive aspects and present themselves in a positive, attractive way. I explained why? They were all superior to Facebook in that they had and were using the latest technology. They were compatible with Facebook's system and would perfectly fit as if they were made with Facebook in mind. Therefore, complementing Facebook in such a way that it would not use all the alleged anticompetitive and bullying or predatory behavior. This is true. Forget the emails and what the CEO said, not because it is not important but because this is what he had in mind. Evidence points to this.

37. Another critical point regarding monopolistic tendencies is the fact that unlike in Standard oil's case where they all are dealing in oil. The same or similar product throughout. The situation is different in the digital world in that with the case at hand. All the new companies Facebook is accused of bullying or pushing out all have different products to

TOMORROW'S WORLD ORDER'S PERSPECTIVE

Facebook in most cases advanced than Facebook's as if upgrades to Facebooks. In that, the technology is different yet complements or augments or enhances Facebook. This is the key.

38. All companies Augmenting and Complementing Facebook to complete one entity in harmony as the final means rather than competing with Facebook as in the meaning of competition.

39. Every company in the digital technology market is not a rivalry, as the oil of Standard Oil is to the oil of the next small company. The way that triggered the antitrust laws.

40. Rather it is many companies that all can complement and fit well with Facebook like I said as they were developed with Facebook in mind or as an improvement to Facebook. This is crucial here. They all fit very well. They are like upgrades to Facebook's platform. They are plug-ins to Facebook. So, the talk of competition and restricting entry or creating barriers is flawed. Yes, they can offer a better way of advertising, etc. But this is not a competition as in antitrust laws. They would rather sell to Facebook than do it as a challenge to Facebook. They all can join and fit into Facebook and create economies of scale as the speed of adverts and other features like better quality pictures or cheaper advertising space might increase benefiting the consumer. The presence of Facebook gives rise to these small startups. They know if they cannot grow to Facebook's level, they can always sell to Facebook lucratively.

41. It is not Facebook's fault that its network has grown that big that others cannot enter the market, so the FTC must break it, so others have chances of making it. This is absurd. Who are they to dictate what a legal entity should do or not do in the context I portrayed above where

Facebook, even though it called these threats, I explained why they could have seen them as threats? No idea at the time that the company arose due to the foresight of the owners in seeing Facebook's shortcomings. Competition and secrecy could have led them not to admit that they created the companies with an indirect goal to sell to Facebook. This is reasonable and open to me to arrive at such a conclusion because they knew Facebook had a social network that centers around a mechanical aspect like photo-sharing as in the lawsuit. They knew all they can do is create a solution now to Facebook's future problems and make a kill as they sell profitably to Facebook. Or they might have realized that the best choice is just to sell to Facebook due to its hard work which earned it the reputation of being the number one. Surely punishing that is outdated and obsolete and cannot be allowed from now on. We will oppose that vehemently.

42. *Facebook's lawsuit page 4.*
43. *12. Facebook initially tried to compete with Instagram on the merits by **improving its mobile photo-sharing features**. [Emphasis added] But by September 2011, Mr. Zuckerberg saw that Facebook had fallen far behind, writing internally: "In the time it has taken us to get our[r] act together on this [,] Instagram has become a large and viable competitor to us on mobile photos, which will increasingly be the future of photos."*

44. I explained in detail what the lawsuit refers to in the quote above. The strategy they adopted is a business model based on the SWOT analysis when dealing with Opportunities. That proves my point that to Facebook even though they agreed or wrote that these were their threats. They were their Opportunities. In business you deal with Opportunities by lining yourself in line with them and by appearing attractive to them, so they see the compatibility and complement part. So, *improving its mobile photo-sharing features* is the matching part. This is different from what Standard Oil did to the smaller companies. Colluding and using the price to create barriers to entry. Facebook is

making it attractive and lets them see why they can complement Facebook. "Getting our act together," is like wooing if this was wooing a woman. It is like matching the opponents and not playing dirty tricks as with the anticompetitive tactics.

45. 13. So Facebook fell back on the philosophy that "it is better to buy than compete." In February 2012, Mr. Zuckerberg acknowledged that if left independent—or in the hands of another acquirer like Google or Apple—Instagram threatened to leave Facebook Blue "very behind in both functionality and brand on how one of the core use cases of Facebook will evolve in the mobile 4 worlds." Emphasizing that this was a "really scary" outcome for Facebook, Mr. Zuckerberg suggested "we might want to consider paying a lot of money" for Instagram.

46. I think the FTC shot themselves in the leg in this quote, that "it is better to buy than compete."

47. Facebook is not buying new startups to kill competition and be the only ones in the game. This is what Standard Oil did. Buyout to freeze out and kick some out and then determine the price they can fix. Facebook is saying this is a survival strategy. revisiting crisis versus risk management arguments I mentioned earlier on and later in the report. It is better to buy the identified Opportunity than to compete with it because they are not the superior but them. They are facing ceasing existence. Rather than looking for ways to gain a large market share. Even though all the strategies are to find a competitive advantage. They saw an Opportunity and not a Threat in Instagram. So, they present themselves well so that the opportunity comes knocking. Paying a lot of money should not be misunderstood as buying out to become a monopoly even though in all circumstance's chances are that they will end up all becoming a monopoly. Their increase in money is to create value for money. Make the deal lucrative become attractive so that they sell. That can trigger other start-ups to start a business just to provide solutions to Facebook. That can kill competition but creates competition unless...

48. INDIRECT KILLING OF COMPETITION BY FACEBOOK THROUGH OFFERING HUGE SUMS TO NEW STARTUPS. BUT HOW CAN THAT BE ANTICOMPETITIVE BEHAVIOR IN THE MEANING OF THE ANTITRUST LAWS.

49. The only conceivable way the FTC can argue that way that Facebook is killing competition is the fact that they can argue that Facebook is offering huge sums of money. Buying out to kill competition in that the startups will start just for Facebook's case. To provide a service and be paid lucratively. That this will fuel a substantial number of short-term small startups that aim to sell to Facebook without long term plans to compete. So, the huge sums of money are to create a short-term boom but without any long-term competition. But it is not Facebook's fault. They are creating competition whether the competition survives or not has nothing to do with Facebook. They are creating competition by offering huge sums. How can that be anticompetitive in the meaning of the antitrust laws?

50. 14. Mr. Zuckerberg recognized that by acquiring and controlling Instagram, Facebook would not only squelch the direct threat that Instagram posed but also significantly hinder another firm from using photo-sharing on mobile phones to gain popularity as a provider of personal social networking. As Mr. Zuckerberg explained to Chief Financial Officer David Ebersman in an email, controlling Instagram would secure Facebook's enduring dominance around one of the few social mechanics that could provide a footing for a competing personal social networking provider:

51. What if Facebook is that "another firm from using photo-sharing on mobile phones to gain popularity as a provider of personal social networking." Because again it is not like the Standard oil case where the product is the same. In the digital technology market, it is different. Facebook did not have this technology in the first place so how can they be hindering another firm when it is a new technology to

TOMORROW'S WORLD ORDER'S PERSPECTIVE

them as well. They have the right to be that new company. They are that new company. Their system had been rendered out of date and obsolete by the arrival of smartphones. Surely that is targeting it just because it has the resources and the large market share. I explained that this is not a risk management exercise but a crisis management one in that the threat is present and real. Whereas the way they are talking is in relation to risk management to gain a competitive advantage. They have a right to buy to survive and be at an advantage. Facebook did not have photo-sharing smartphone messaging.

52. The passage quoted by the FTC defends Facebook.

53. [T]here are network effects around social products and **a finite number of different social mechanics to invent**. [**Emphasis added**] Once someone **wins at a specific mechanic, it is difficult** [critical phrase here] for others to supplant them without doing something different. It is possible someone beats Instagram by building something better to the point that they get network migration, but this is harder if Instagram keeps running as a product. [Integrating Instagram's functions into Facebook] is also a factor but, we already know these companies' social dynamics and will integrate them over the next 12-24 months anyway. **The integration plan involves building their mechanics into our products rather than directly integrating their products {Emphasis added]** if that makes sense. . .. page 5.

54. Entry as a competitor is difficult due to *the **finite number of different social mechanics to invent**. [**Emphasis added**] Once someone **wins at a specific mechanic, it is difficult**]* for others to supplant them without doing something different. Entry is difficult not because of Facebook's anticompetitive tactics no. But the very nature of the digital technology market. This is augmented by the fact that since 2011 in the USA there has been any major entry to challenge Facebook's position. Simply because the nature of the market makes entry difficult unless totally different from Facebook's.

55. That defends my analysis that to Facebook all these companies are Opportunities to them and not threats. The way they dealt with them are ways not in the jurisdiction of the antitrust anticompetitive tactics. I will explain why.

56. First, this is not the Standard oil situation where the product is the same. We are dealing with dynamic digital and technological environments here. Based on a single invention. Mechanism of social networking through photo and messaging services. That there is no other way.

57. [T]here are network effects around social products and **a finite number of different social mechanics to invent**. Page 5.

58. Again, as I have argued, Facebook because of its early invention of social mechanics, everyone else came to existence as a way of complementing and integrating with Facebook. Facebook in this light is the trigger rather than the killer of competition and the rise of these small entities. It is because of Facebook's gifted status of finding a way that is near the only way to communicate so that everyone else centers around them. Surely you cannot be serious to suggest that such intelligence of the CEO is a crime that fits under the antitrust laws. That will kill innovation and incentives to invest. ***If there were other potential companies, they would have established themselves by now since then***. But the finite nature of the invention means it is possible for the next 5 to 10 years that there will not be another rivalry to Facebook. So, the talk about anticompetitive tactics is not just flawed but an attack on the fundamental principles that surround the company laws. That a corporation as a legal entity cannot be interfered with without suing back as the image is everything and these lawsuits can adversely affect the shares and valuation of a company. We will draft laws to

TOMORROW'S WORLD ORDER'S PERSPECTIVE

use to sue greedy lazy interstate and agencies like the FTC who patiently wait to make a kill through dodge accusations and use of obsolete laws with the view of becoming the $billion spenders see $billion congress below. The regulatory burden and unlawful fines are a huge obstacle to the realization of economies of scale. Just like these are tough on dodgy corporations and trusts. We will be tough with dodgy governments who steal through outdated laws from hard-working genuine firms. To go to the next stage of development it is only through the facilitation of these corporations so that they realize economies of scale. Then offer the highest quality products at cheaper prices. Triggering huge wealth and better lifestyles for all. This is the way forward. Just see how big they have grown. Look at Amazon. Now we must assume they have a responsibility to take all humanity out of this poor stage. Who else can help humanity do that? The FTC? Or The interstate? Please. They are dealing with their crisis management plan right now as we speak. One that centers around Facebook for easy $billion to spend lavishly hence the collection and ganging up of all interstates etc. to bring a lawsuit against Facebook. To make things worse. Facebook is their only way out. A huge check in this pandemic striking environment will alleviate all their problems. This is not about the antitrust laws as they want you to think. This is about first their crisis management planning that focuses on Facebook. Secondly, it is about their falling tariffs collected figures. This is about dealing with the pandemic as well. This is about their drying out coffers. This is about the political aspect of Facebook especially its influence or potential impact in American politics its role or perceived impact in the 2020 elections. Why raise the issues now when this happened in 2012 and 2014? When they approved everything. Does this herald or point to the need for a new world order platform in Tomorrow's World Order? Surely there must now be a referee or a judge between the big corporations especially the tech giants and the FTC, the Department of Justice, and the interstates. The antitrust laws had benefits to people in mind at the core exacerbated by the then-recent slavery trauma that is in 1890. But this is 2021 and the system has become very unfair and the once judges have become the vehicles of creating even more harm to the consumers and the business at large. We as a global political party have discovered that when everyone else talked about abolishing slavery, etc., and bring all this into law. Little do people know that it was only because they had found an even technologically advanced way of doing the same things. But now they are using digital technology to create software and miniature plane parts that they can use to do all kinds of the evil they are accusing the hard-working corporations of doing.

59. Governments, etc. as doing exactly what they are accusing the corporation but secretly using technology and drone software remotely to steal and spy stealing information and trading this to the highest bidders.

60. Yes, you will be shocked that human hacking triggered the abolishing of slavery as a better-undetected form. They are deliberately hacking one in 50 and as much as one in 30 from the ethnic minority and categorizing them as either disabled, mentally unstable, or as having learning difficulties to cover themselves but all these have spying devices, they use to twin phone screens and computers of everyone within a certain radius. Then steal ideas using video senders, etc. to check everything. To cover themselves, they pretend they are the ones guiding that

person that they recreate that issue. But then sell the ideas for donations, etc., and then use radiation through the technology implanted at birth without the people's consent to kill that person with cancers, etc. to get rid of the evidence, etc. So, who is harming here?

61. Anticompetitive behavior refers to what they are doing. Using snooping tactics to know all conversations. They use their delayed time-space continuum mechanism that states that whatever happens at a point in time. It takes seconds to reach the satellite and be redirected back to the same place. Meaning if you are in the office having a secret conversation. After you have left someone can go to that place and listen to all your conversation if one of them was in the vicinity recording. They can playback and then know what happened at the meeting. Then try to pretend they are guiding the people. Be wary of their development packages. Ways of sinking you in debt using this technology and GPS functions to control the outcomes of business meetings and deals over time that you are guaranteed to go bankrupt through advanced grooming. Encouraging new start-ups to take huge loans then control the income they get until a time they cannot repay the loan they then offer them protection. Meaning having their hairs grayed faster. Getting themselves edged faster. Ask me why? So that they can get back their money from your life insurance, they age you faster, so you die early, and they have their money back when you die. They might split you up or kill your partner but give you one of theirs before you die to collect all your life insurance. If you know what these can do, you would support us to bring laws to deal with these and not corporations.

62. After all, I argued below that they have a misconception of business and free markets. Are you surprised most do not have a business degree and have basic education trained

though by the system just as a chicken birth will always be an egg? Whatever they learn will be what they are supposed to learn and do. Imagine these laws they use today are the same laws created in 1890. No offense but surely a lot of things have changed since.

63. Do you know why they hang on to these obsolete outdated laws and institutions?
64. They secretly recreate the conditions then using all kinds of secret slavery hacks. Hacking, torture, manipulating, etc., and all kinds of evil. The real reason why they are strict with the tech giants is that this is one area they cannot control directly so their protective methods do not work.

65. THE $BILLION CONGRESS. THE REASONS BEHIND THE TOUGH CRACKDOWN OF TECH GIANTS LIKE FACEBOOK, ETC. BY THE FTC, INTERSTATE, AND DEPARTMENT OF JUSTICE.

66. This is because this digital technology introduced an element they cannot control. They have managed to control business, etc. simply because they have a physical address and can track and manipulate who goes there and what time and how much they get as revenue, etc. But the rise of the internet and technology meant an increase in human hacking at the same time as the invention of the internet. To match and find a way of still controlling everything. The reason being the lucrative fines to corporations and trusts that can fill their coffers. The very reason all interstates came to get. Picture wild dogs hunting or piranhas feasting? Yes, that is more like it. All coming together is declaring their share of the fine. A money-making tool. Do you know at the time the Sherman

TOMORROW'S WORLD ORDER'S PERSPECTIVE

Act was enacted the government at the time was referred to as the **billion-dollar congress**? The Act was put in place simply to increase the revenues and increase tariff collections to increase federal spending? You will see that all their fines are in tune of billion dollars. The very reasons they gang up together. The very act they discourage others and call this monopoly grouping to fix prices to control the market and here they do the same. The very fact they grouped is so that they fix the fines. The $billion-dollar club. Money that is to be misused and used not for business but to hold everyone as slaves through illegal surveillance. Spying technology used to be ahead of the game in hacking, torturing, and spying.

67. Ladies and gentlemen these are the very reasons why we are fighting the system and calling for a better system that values the people. To us, abolishing must mean just that. We stand firm to stop this practice of taking money to further make things to further abuse the people. If the money was used for community projects, etc., we would not defend rich corporations like Facebook.

68. Our grievances are that they make it easy to be sued and fined giving money away easily. If it was used for the betterment of humanity, it was better. This money can never be tracked or have someone voice where it was spent. This is the very money used to enslave and abuse humankind. That is why they say to themselves or some of them that corporations are evil. They are funding illegal government activities by giving them easy money. Remember the Trusts that collected tariffs so that they build huge boats to carry as many slaves as they can? This is still the case only that the government is doing this through fines. Once they are found out they start saying corporations are evil and should not be let to grow that way simply because they will pay fines easily leaving the

government with no option but to engage in illegal activities such as illegal hacking and spying or surveillance.

69. CORPORATIONS INVOLVED IN THE SECRET HACKING TOO AS ACCOMPLICES.

70. Today's corporations know governments are human hacking their people and deliberately do stupid things like breaching privacy rules. Knowing the government will try to sue them publicly and win. But then go on secretly to develop human hacking technology or hack everyone so that the corporations then use these to track and trace and snoop on their activities so that they have the accurate data that they use to sell, say advertising slots, or generate audiences for the business. Governments own satellites, etc. they use too. So, the fines are like an indirect fee for spying services.

71. ANTITRUST FINES AS FEES FOR USING ILLEGAL TECHNOLOGY AND FOR VIOLATING GOVERNMENT'S COPYRIGHTS. GOVERNMENTS AS SNOOPING SPICES.

72. Governments of today are advanced than most corporations because what a government can do under the national security theme the corporations cannot do the same. The effectiveness of data, etc. is important in the social networking arena. Governments are still using secret slavery in most cases without the people knowing. The tech giants snoop or find out by inviting everyone to write books on their platform. Meaning a way of reporting. Picture a woman holding a secret from her husband but confessing it to the pastor at church through the confession act saying, "Father forgive me I have sinned. It

has been these days," etc. Now the pastor alone knows a secret about this woman, but the trust placed in him means only he can keep the secret. But the husband has seen his wife going to the church and suspects that the wife might have confided in the pastor. But he cannot accuse the pastor of keeping secrets. So, he threatens to find the pastor guilty of things not related to the case. He might look at other antitrust acts that discredit his credibility but there is little he can do in this case because the pastor is not using this information for his private gains. But just for the church. So, the husband might not act. Now imagine a case where the pastor uses that information to start a personal business that benefits him. Surely the husband and his friends who might be going through the same issues with their wives might group and sue that business. The pastor cannot protest much. He might give them money to keep the secret and carry on with the business. Meaning entering a partnership where he keeps using the secrets maybe now for everyone to make huge profits and as a way of paying for copyright etc. then do something stupid to anger the husband so that they sue publicly his company. Then he pays the huge fines as fees for continued use of the secrets. Both are gaining so that keeps the relationship of suing and paying forever. The people are the ones who suffer. At first, they went to the government when their privacy was breached and complained. The corporation was sued, but the money was used to further silence them through increased hacking, secret torture, etc. Now they cannot prove it but know that the government is eviler than the corporation. Because the government raped you first by letting the doctor drug you heavily during say a pandemic-related test and implant things but without cutting you but firing a needle diode into your body. A needle they will activate remotely like a drone. They then use electromagnetic nerve tampering. Picture dog collars emitting electricity. That diode now in your buttocks or arm, etc. has also GPS properties to pinpoint exactly where you are. It has recording or microphone properties, etc. In most cases, you never know.

73. The only reason that made you know that you have something is when you bought a PS2 PlayStation or a Nintendo with a wireless remote. You are playing a racing or rally game Need for Speed with your mates that somehow the controller jams up. You change the frequency but now you feel vibrations within you. You look everywhere maybe you are sitting on a remote or phone, etc. You discovered that it is something within you. You freaked out. Then with time after researching you start reading about the CIA doing all kinds of spying on their enemies, etc. Then you recall maybe it was only through birth you get those things as you never had an operation. Now you are skeptical of the government. You have no one to turn to. You report to an international organization. Then your life is turned upside down. You hear there is a big corporation with power enough to cause the government to piss itself. You smile and write to them. Get video proof and everything and send it to their platform where they publish it live for all to see. The government is finished you might think. But then the corporation makes a huge profit. They start using the hackings as well secretly. The time the governments find out they go mad and group all of them. As this threatens the fabric of their existence. They launch a case against the corporations but not after fines but after fees for suing and continued use in billion dollars. The only player in this scenario suffering is the consumer. The corporations now grow even bigger using everyone who is hacked to make out-of-this-world profits.

TOMORROW'S WORLD ORDER'S PERSPECTIVE

The government cannot stop them as they are the origin of the source. The only thing they can do now is using some stupid laws that were supposed to be scraped but kept to give them cover. Now it is time to collect the fees. All this time the consumer is being fucked by all. The fine money never reaches the victims instead is used to buy more radiation doses to keep those who might complain quieted or silence by death through cancers etc. Now the entire world must be hacked. They are now creating man-made bio e.g. the pandemic with the aim to hack everyone in the name of testing and serum-based vaccines used full of live viruses that will make one require an operation in the future or digital ones later used to ask people to be tested and on testing a thin diode the size of a needle is fired into the body. Picture a nail gun in operation which is then used to control that person. It is a big business. The tech is growing fast because they are using banned secret slavery techniques. Guess what? They are partnerships with the government as the fines are fees for copyrights use and use of the hacking devices, etc. Guess what everyone is? Government property and not citizens.

74. You bloody cannot stand the truth!

75. I know at the time of writing this is a controversial topic but years to come will prove me right. Humanity only accepts the truth when something has happened. So, in this case, the people are the victims. But it is not all hopeless as we are now operating globally. Welcome to Tomorrow's World Order.

76. GOVERNMENT'S SNOOPING AND ACTING AS SPIES. CONVERTING CITIZEN'S THOUGHTS TO TEXT TO HELP CORPORATIONS IN ITS ANALYSIS OF DATA.

77. The government has used secret technology usually found in military circles on its citizens through hacking and now

sells information to businesses about what people are thinking. Yes, what people are thinking. Brain mapping and electromagnetic reconnaissance and the study of the brain to know which parts react and what areas of the brain are highlighted have made governments create advanced ways of reading the people's thoughts and now sell the information to the corporations in return for huge exorbitant fines as fees for use. It is now easy to know what a person is thinking if that person is hacked. A computer converts the thoughts to text and then the message is given for example, to corporations, etc. to do business, etc. Advanced spying methods. With accuracy levels above ninety percent of exactly what the person is thinking.

78. THE POSSIBLE ALTERNATIVE TO FACEBOOK IS DIGIBOOK MY INVENTION.

79. What the FTC should be doing is encouraging other ways. The digital electromagnetic message is a possibility. Where feelings and everything like visual or say the changes, you feel say if something moves fast in front of you can be the future a rivalry to Facebook. But that requires serious technological advances as people can communicate digitally. Talking in their heads silently and a machine or smartphone being able to use brain-reading imaging techniques to interpret exactly what that person is saying and then convert to the word. As thoughts to word then another reads the converted message back to digital making the other person feel what the message is about digitally by feeling e.g., feelings of hunger or arousal, etc. Being able to send a picture in one's head and that converted to an image and then back to the image as the person sees the image in his eyes just by the reception of

the digital electromagnetic rays, etc. Then people can simply place the advert with Digibook which then sends digital messages as digital advertisements to the brain.

80. 15. On April 9, 2012—the day Facebook announced it was acquiring Instagram—Mr. Zuckerberg wrote privately to a colleague to celebrate suppressing the threat: "I remember your internal post about how Instagram was our threat and not Google+. You were right. One thing about startups though is you can often acquire them."

81. That proves my point that the CEO might have not known or considered Instagram as an opportunity and not a threat. Even if they were in the harshest sense. The way they dealt with these is not threatening to make Instagram be a threat to justify using the antitrust laws on them. Yes, they might have seen them as a threat because of the unknown and secrecy nature of businesses closed to competitors, etc. But the method employed of matching and lining with them and to treat them positively offering lucrative deals is a way done only to Opportunities rather than Threats. Read what Standard oil did to the smaller firms to differentiate an Opportunity one showing the attractiveness of a corporation like Facebook and the other forced to exit and ended operations by Standard Oil.

82. Note that the current system or stage; the one sought after by the FTC and the other agencies are in the Early Stage of Development. Characterized by.

83. Many players most of which make an only profit to stay in business.

84. Most provide lower prices products simply because they are of poor quality as compared to the ones that can be provided by a large corporation that has achieved economies of scale.

85. There are no incentives to invest as they do not make enough profits.

86. There are many players yes simply because most sell a similar poor-quality product

87. Most are in business waiting for the right time to sell to a big tech giant like Facebook. That brings me to the next point. Most small companies came into being only so that they will sell to the big tech giant when the time comes.

88. No matter how the FTC, government agencies, and Interstates do not want to hear this. It is a business model to create a company to sell it to the tech giant when the price is right, and the time is perfect. It is a misunderstood concept. You have the FTC, and their antitrust laws talk about anticompetitive allegations, etc. but no one ever accepts that possibility and this being a big likelihood. Instagram and WhatsApp might have been started as a business to be sold to Facebook anywhere. Or a business idea started with selling it to a tech giant at some point when the offered price is right. I know of a model that creates a business to sell to the tech giants at the right time. So, it is also true that if this is the case Facebook cannot be accused of anticompetitive practices of buying their smaller rivals when the rivals were created with them in mind. Here if that is the case Facebook is doing these smaller companies a favor. Making them realize the initial goal. Of selling the company off to Facebook. So, there is no harm being done to smaller businesses or competition here. The tech giant is doing good. Meaning the FTC and the Department of Justice are the ones here doing harm.

89. Anticompetitive Conditioning. In addition to its strategy of acquiring competitive threats to its social networking monopoly, Facebook has, over many years, announced and enforced anticompetitive conditions on access to its valuable platform interconnections, such as the application programming interfaces ("APIs") that it makes available to third-party software applications. Page 7.

90. Facebook, as argued above is the trigger of all the small new startups as complementing it. That means all these

startups joined the Facebook platform as they arose to complete it rather than compete with it. After all, they volunteered to join as this is the only one to use as Facebook invented the social networking mechanism. Until they invented theirs there is little they can do because there are no other ways. So, this cannot amount to anti-competitive acts.

91. The talk of harm to competition is nonsense.

92. This is the digital technological area where there is one invention that makes everyone else start up a business with one aim. To sell it to Facebook at a lucrative price. There is no other goal. This was the idea behind the start-up. Over 16 years now and there has not been another massive alternative in the US meaning that it is not easy and that cannot amount to:

93. Harm to Competition. Through at least the foregoing conduct, Facebook suppresses, deters, hinders, and eliminates personal social networking competition, and maintains its monopoly power in the U.S. personal social networking market, through means other than merits competition. In doing so, Facebook deprives users of personal social networking in the United States of the benefits of competition, including increased choice, quality, and innovation. 8 Facebook cannot justify this substantial harm to competition with claimed efficiencies, procompetitive benefits, or business justifications that could not be achieved through other means. Page 8.

ABILITY TO INVENT SOMETHING WHERE NO ONE CAN FIND AN ALTERNATIVE DOES NOT AMOUNT TO HARM TO COMPETITION.

94. 1. Facebook's Anticompetitive Conditions on Platform Access Required Developers Not to Work with Competitors

95. May 2014: Platform 3.0 launches. A new approach—dubbed Platform 3.0—launched on May 2, 2014. At that time, Facebook terminated all apps' access to certain APIs, which included restricting third-party apps from accessing information about their users' friends who were not already using that third-party app.

This can be viewed in line with data breaches and privacy concerns. Allowing other users and competitors links will only result in invasions of privacy to third party friends whom Facebook are also responsible for. I think bearing in mind that on this issue I might be wrong because the reason could be

CEO specific for doing so. But bearing in mind that they were fined record fines up to $5 billion surely you can't be surprised especially knowing the issue about Cambridge Analytica.

The FTC had been probing allegations political consultancy Cambridge Analytica **improperly obtained the data of up to 87 million Facebook users**. The probe then widened to include other issues such as facial recognition. The $5bn fine is believed to be the biggest ever imposed on any company for violating consumers' privacy.
BBC 24 July 2019. https://www.bbc.co.uk/news/business-49099364

"Despite repeated promises to its billions of users worldwide that they could control how their personal information is shared, Facebook undermined consumers' choices," said FTC Chairman Joe Simons.

96. We might never know but this could be the reason behind what now the same agency is regarding as "Facebook's Anticompetitive Conditions on Platform Access Required Developers Not to Work with Competitors."

97. This looks suspect that the same agency on the one hand they are crying foul play on the part of Facebook that they are misusing the people data and leaving their gates open to the third party. The very way the Cambridge Analytical case obtained the data through third parties. Now it is crying foul play that they are blocking the same third party responsible for leaking the data. That always creates more questions than answers. Is there more to it than we are meant to believe?

98. But Cambridge Analytica was not the only firm to have access to users' data - **the data was gathered using Facebook's infrastructure at that time,** [Emphasis Added.] and many other developers had taken advantage of it without authorization.

99. **Facebook was fined £500,000 by the UK's data protection watchdog** for its role in the Cambridge Analytica data scandal in October.

100. The fact that when there is a breach the government is paid and not the victims are suspects. Such practices fuel

secret abuse by the government selling access rights using methods that are illegal like hacking. The more the corporation pays the more the abuse continues. Something we as the new global leaders are against. We will do our best. That if something does not seem right then we will investigate and punish both governments and corporations and directly pay the victims from the fines collected rather than what is going on. Where the money is invested to make even more secret and lethal hacks.

101.   Here we see Facebook following the government's use of trying to illegally impose facial recognition and use it to breach people's rights.

102. **Confirming previous reports**, the FTC found that certain Facebook policies violated rules against deceptive practices. For instance, it said Facebook's data policy was deceptive to people who **used its facial recognition tool**.
103. The social network also fell afoul of the regulator by not revealing that phone numbers collected for two-factor authentication would be used for advertising.
104. BBC 24 July 2019
105. Shareholders seeking to halt Amazon's sale of its facial recognition technology to US police forces have been defeated in two votes that sought to pressure the company into a rethink.
106. Civil rights campaigners had said it was "perhaps the most dangerous surveillance technology ever developed,"
107. BBC 22 May 2019

108. Facebook's Enforcement of its Anticompetitive Conditions Deterred Emerging Threats.
109. Lawsuit page 45.

110.   This can be in relation to the data and privacy issues rather than to competition. You will find that it is a thin line between being open enough and protecting the data and privacy of the users. You let third party access then you have a privacy issue. I think all these arguments about restricting others and trade have weakened the FTC's case that it needs throwing out of the window. This is because

of the heavy fine Facebook paid. Surely probably the highest ever fine paid to date. That will make Facebook think again about this competition thing and whether to allow access to third parties the very method exploited.

111.   THE TRICKERY, DEVIOUS AND MANIPULATING ACTS OF THE FTC.

112.   Again, we find the FTC not playing fair. But poking Facebook in the ass and as they turn around to look who is doing this, then poke Facebook again in the ass but on the other side as two of them take turns. How can Facebook protect itself from the FTC's lawsuits about anticompetitive practices and at the same time deal with privacy and data abuse issues? Surely being fined that kind of money would put 99.9% of the firms and corporations out of business. The environment can be said to be against corporations who might be afraid to say the real issues for fear of being further victimized. Or the other reason is that they have benefited from illegal data, data breaches, and privacy concerns before, and now they cannot fight the government and are being blackmailed.

113.   FINES OR FEES?

114.   It sounds like what I highlighted above where the government starts abusing the citizens using software that has not been consented to. Then corporations do the same then the government steps in to fine them and the corporation helping them to win as well. Is it a secret but public way to pay for rights to use and or copyright of illegally obtained permissions that are illegal anywhere? You should see how they defend the corporations like they are the Kingpin who collects money from them and offers them Protection services. The hacking I am talking about is used to give people unique features but all artificial. E.g., one open eye than the other, etc., or a dodgy-looking one

strand of gray hair or some dodgy laughing, etc. Proofs that they are the ones behind him or supporting him. But also, a victim of the hacking I mentioned above. That they snooped and spied on that person and stole the ideas and to be recognized or to collect fees then pretend to guide that person.

115.   The world is still a dark place and we have a lot to do. Welcome, all to Tomorrow's World Order.

116.   THE TALK OF HARM TO COMPETITION IS FLAWED.

117. VIII. HARM TO COMPETITION 161. Through the conduct described above, Facebook has hindered, suppressed, and deterred the emergence and growth of rival personal social networking providers, and unlawfully maintained its monopoly in the U.S. personal social networking market, other than through merits competition. 162. The conduct described above harmed and continues to harm, competition by limiting and suppressing competition that Facebook otherwise would have to face in provision 47 of personal social networking. networking. Lawsuit page 47.

118.   This is flawed in the digital and technology market because the methods and mechanics might not be replicated. Innovation to provide a better alternative might be hard to come by. Most of the players that will start-up are there just to complement Facebook and join its platform as an upgrade because there is no alternative. The business model is to provide Facebook with a better solution to the current method at a high selling price. Simply as that. The fact that since 2007 there has not been a major competitor to Facebook in the US diminishes the strength of this accusation. It simply means there is no competition because it can never exist at least or the coming years so until then the FTC has no right to sue Facebook. It has nothing to do with Facebook's approach. They created a unique mechanical means of social networking that cannot be alternated. Simply put. Everyone else interested can only startup to complement

rather than compete. Mind you this is not the Standard oil case. Where Standard oil can create barriers. Here a clever and advanced innovation is the barrier creator. Surely you cannot penalize people for that.

119. As a result, users of personal social networking in the United States have been deprived of the benefits of additional competition for personal social. Lawsuit page 47.

120.   Yes, it is true, but this has nothing to do with Facebook even if it did the fact that no alternative exists in the US means it is possibly impossible. This is the barrier to entry, not Facebooks' acts.

121.   ROLE OF ECONOMIES OF SCALE.

122.   I think in the digital world and technology it is a misconception that quality is compromised by the merger of corporations. The talk of improved quality with the competition is flawed. A big misconception. Mergers create the best way to increase quality at very lower prices this is true. It is wrong to think many players as competitors will increase the quality of products be it advertising space, etc. This is wrong showing misunderstandings of how the business operates. Competition in this area and sector cannot be competition for the sake of it. More players mean a reduced market share as everyone fights for a slice. There are no incentives to invest. The competitors and everyone end up making just enough to stay afloat. Where do they get the money to improve quality? Those who do have to invest heavily in research and development will push others out thereby creating monopolistic conditions. That brings things to the same stage we are in where there is one big player with a huge market share. Who will merge with others to reduce cost due to economies of scale? That in turn means more

money for quality improvement at less cost. So, there is real quality at reduced prices. The quality where there are many competitors is not the same when the corporation has realized its economies of scale. Quantity is not quality. The prices can never be the same. Look, big companies can afford to sell below market prices where it is dominant. This is because they worry about the market share first which will mean a return on investment in the future as they start making profits. Look at the growth of Amazon as a good example. Why it keeps growing is that it can create real quality at lower prices by reducing fees, etc. something a large competitive bunch would not do.

123.   IT IS THE INTERSTATE'S SURVIVAL STRATEGY RATHER THAN CALLS TO INCREASE COMPETITION.

124. 164. In addition, by monopolizing the U.S. market for personal social networking, Facebook also harmed, and continues to harm, competition for the sale of advertising in the United States. Because personal social networking providers typically monetize through the sale of advertising, Facebook's suppression of competing personal social networking providers also has enabled Facebook to avoid close competition in the supply of advertising services. 165. Competing personal social networking providers would have been close competitors of Facebook Blue in the supply of advertising. This is because they would have been able to offer the distinctive advertising features described above that distinguish social advertising from other forms of display advertising, search advertising, and "offline" advertising.

125. Page 48.

126.   There are no other ways that are clearer to the real motives of all these interstates and the government in this lawsuit than that Facebook is squeezing the coffers too. Since Facebook has grown rapidly, it has become the only lucrative form of advertising. The acquisitions of WhatsApp and Instagram have meant reduced advertising revenue of other forms namely I quote, "display advertising, search advertising, and "offline" advertising.

127.   This is advertising that was once the mainstream
before Facebook came into play or bought the other two.
That has meant reduced revenues and or lower tariffs or
fees collected from these to match Facebook fees on
advertising. We are dealing with chickens and cows here.
Facebook is universal and does not need to be tied to a
physical address. The very form that once was the highest
earner for interstates. Now they have bills to pay like the
electricity they use to light electronic billboards etc. yet
the revenues are dwindling. Facebook here is the culprit. It
is more effective as well. There is real-time information
about the activity of the advertising whereas this lacks
physical advertising alternatives. What the lawsuit is about
is going back to the time when billboards etc. were the
best form of advertising. What other Facebook alternatives
will use display advertising and offline advertising that are
new and can compete with Facebook? This is part of the
government's systematic way of dealing with change.
Rollback to the most profitable time, methods, and
techniques even if they are outdated. This is the case with
secret slavery etc. This was the cheapest and most
profitable means, so now they take money through fines
from these corporations to recreate the same conditions
through hacking and digital weapons. Now they are asking
for the courts to Rollback Facebook to times they
benefited the most. Surely no wonder why we are still in
the defense stages of development. Read Tomorrow's
World Order.

128.   We stand strongly against the current system and
this kind of thinking of breaking things and rolling all back
as in Rollback just because you cannot stand change or
that change will put you out of business.

129.   It is time to break these useless institutions. All of
them and put a new system fit for us as we are the leaders

of tomorrow. It is time to call for these big corporations to Fund us so that we can help not just them but everyone, especially the people. The very people who are victims of all being taken turns to be abused with the government covering their tracks by further victimizing the victims using the police and hospitals, etc. The corporations must Fund Tomorrow's World Order so that we can implement our system. We have rights to our currency, and this will be a great investment for them. We can put new laws to facilitate further developments but on conditions that the corporations take more what are the government's jobs. More housing. The building of cities, etc. Involved in new technology even if not related to their corporation but simply because they have the money and power to do so. But they are still answerable to us. **The use of illegal hacking and torture and everything associated with the current system renders them unfit and must be wound up and Rolled down the drain with immediate effect**. Drag all to court and charge with a list of charges.

130.   Involved in abolished practices. Outright calls to break up this forever. I have seen companies destroyed for lesser crimes. It is time we end these useless institutions still enslaving the people.

131.   Torture is abolished and or forbidden by international laws. Hacking makes one if found guilty have a three-life sentence or instant death as hacking is evil and synonymous with slavery. A hacker is a murderer hacking to change often healthy functions to kill. He is also a torturer as he is no better than a slave master. He is a hostage-taker because a hacked person has no legal rights as he or she is a hostage of the hacker. A hacker is a violator of human rights worse than the slave master and the pirate before him.

132.   A VICIOUS CYCLE OF ABUSE.

133.   The governments are big violators of competition snooping secretly and spying. Governments are letting once military technology in the society and doing what they used to do to prisoners of war now doing this to their citizens for a fee giving vital information to these big giants especially tech giants to growing significantly through breaches of the people's privacy etc. To make things worse with not even a single victim compensated but instead the money used to make even more useless and secret gadgets to breach rights even harder. If this climate of abuse and corruption exists, the breaches and fines will keep growing.

134.   Our system will reward the victims even if that means bankrupting these. To us, it is not about the fees, but the methods used. Most breach and violate the fabric on which the rights are based. Creating situations when if we do not act, they both will take all citizens back to slavery or worse but secretly.

135.   Stand with us to block the huge fines unless they are plowing them back into projects that benefit the victims. Urge the corporations that it is good to donate to us; Tomorrow's World Order; as we have everyone's interests at heart.

136. IX. VIOLATION OF LAW Monopolization of Personal Social Networking Arising Under Section 2 of the Sherman Act 169. The FTC re-alleges and incorporates by reference the allegations in paragraphs 1- 167 above. 170. At least since 2011, Facebook has had monopoly power in the United States concerning personal social networking. 171. Facebook has willfully maintained its monopoly power through its course of anticompetitive conduct, including through anticompetitive acquisitions and anticompetitive conditioning of access to interconnections. Through its course of conduct, Facebook has excluded competition and willfully maintained its monopoly in personal social networking through means other than competing on the merits. 172. Facebook's course of conduct is ongoing. Facebook continues to hold and integrate the competitive threats it acquired in Instagram and WhatsApp. Facebook recognizes that its continued ownership and operation of Instagram

TOMORROW'S WORLD ORDER'S PERSPECTIVE

and WhatsApp both neutralizes their direct competitive threats and creates and maintains a "moat" that protects Facebook from entry into personal social networking by another firm via mobile photo-sharing and mobile messaging. Facebook continues to monitor the industry for competitive threats, and likely would seek to acquire any companies that constitute, or could be repositioned to constitute, threats to its social networking monopoly. Further, having suspended its anticompetitive platform policies in response to anticipated public scrutiny, Facebook is likely to reinstitute such policies or equivalent measures when such scrutiny passes. 173. There is no procompetitive justification for Facebook's exclusionary conduct in maintaining its personal social networking monopoly.

137.   I have dealt much with the Sherman Act as an out-of-date law. To be fair the conditions in which it was enacted have greatly changed unless if they are basing the fact that they have secretly recreated the same conditions through human hacking etc. to justify that. Then still where such uses exist that triggers call to make sure that such a government ceases to exist in the slightest meaning of the phrase. The crime is so grave that a corporation like Facebook can help us prove the same as they have the technology and money and have been given a lot of secrets through their book or video platforms that we can take action against a government still doing this. Abolishing evil practices must mean just that.

138.   The Sherman Act was enacted in line with a normal corporation. I have argued throughout how unfitting it can be used by digital high-tech giants. This is not Standard oil. Care must be taken in dealing with this Sherman Act. We are against obstructive regulatory burdens. The judge must put more emphasis not on the Sherman Act but the intention of the FTC and its agencies etc. The question to answer here is; Is all this is for the good of the people or their survival? The harm to people of their acts as I have highlighted here as compared to those of corporations who do the most harm?

139.   Now that I have highlighted the personal interests and the clash of interests here it is no longer fair to let

these two deals with these. The arguments are that a referee in Tomorrow's World Order is needed for a fair judgment. They both have abused the consumer leaking data and snooping illegally. We cannot trust any to have the people's interests. That justifies Tomorrow's World Order's presence and its active role.

140.   A GRANT OF A RELIEF THAT IS USED TO FURTHER ABUSE THE VICTIMS IS NO RELIEF AT ALL.

141. IX. POWER TO GRANT RELIEF 175. Section 13(b) of the FTC Act, 15 U.S.C. § 53(b), empowers this Court to issue a permanent injunction against violations of the FTC Act and, in the exercise of its equitable jurisdiction, to order equitable relief to remedy the injury caused by Facebook's violations.

142.   I have proved above that all this is a business deal between the states and the corporations. Where illegally the state collects information by hacking everyone, then lets the corporations use the information so that they gain considerable. Then come back to penalize it through fines. It then uses the money to make even more sophisticated ways of snooping and surveillance all of which is wrong. We do not and must not reward evil practices. Better compensate the victims the very people who are having a bad experience.

143.   WHERE THE GOVERNMENT DOES THE SAME TO ITS CITIZENS, IT HAS NO RECOURSE TO THE ARGUMENT OF A RELIEF.

144. X. PRAYER FOR RELIEF WHEREFORE, the FTC requests that this Court, as authorized by Section 13(b) of the FTC Act, 15 U.S.C. § 53(b), and according to its equitable powers, enter final judgment against Facebook, declaring, ordering, and adjudging: A. that Facebook's course of conduct, as alleged herein, violates Section 2 of the Sherman Act and thus constitutes an unfair method of competition in violation of Section 5(a) of the FTC Act, 15 U.S.C. § 45(a).

TOMORROW'S WORLD ORDER'S PERSPECTIVE

145.   TALKING OF OUTDATED LAWS.

146.   The context is misunderstood. Digital technology is different and must be interpreted with caution. What applied to the Sherman Act will not apply to Facebook. The acts of the FTC that are themselves predatory are the ones causing Facebook to react the way they are. It has not done something directly or indirectly to become a monopoly apart from inventing a method that will put them in that position. The so-called anticompetitive behavior is in line with heavy fines to deal with privacy issues rather than anticompetitive behavior. The FTC cannot be trusted as it has become a pain for big industries calling for the breakup and Rollbacks to recreate times and conditions when they collected heavy tariffs. **Do you know that at the time of the Sherman Act's enactment Congress at the time was referred to as the $billion-dollar congress because of the huge tariffs?** The Sherman Act is a levy collecting tool that is so unfair and to us obsolete. For the court to rely on this Act is not just a miscarriage of justice. But an act that can threaten the fabric of human existence because the money is used to develop snooping methods to provide surveillance and collect more information that is sold by these agencies using techniques synonymous to slavery or having slavery connotations.

147.   It is a fact that all companies in this market can only complement Facebook rather than provide a competitive environment. So, Facebook is the trigger of all these companies. The huge prices it pays says it all. It rewards startups that benefit themselves. This is a business model authorized by the companies act. The fact that Facebook under the company's Act the act that gave it life and cannot be found guilty by such laws. Is evidence that it has operated lawfully and legally in its dealings with the competition. All the above allegations in the lawsuits are

witch hunts. They feel that way because the Sherman Act
was enacted to collect high tariffs. The main aim of all their
lawsuits with Facebook.

148. **Facebook will pay a record $5bn fine to settle privacy concerns, the US
Federal Trade Commission (FTC) has said.**
149. The social network must also establish an independent privacy committee that
Facebook's chief executive Mark Zuckerberg will not have control over.
150. The FTC had been probing allegations political consultancy Cambridge
Analytica **improperly obtained the data of up to 87 million Facebook users**.
151. BBC 24 July 2019

152.   THE BILLION DOLLAR FTC V THE BILLION DOLLAR
CONGRESS.

153. **Definition and Summary of the Billion Dollar Congress**
Summary and Definition: The 51st Congress, was given the derisive name
'Billion Dollar Congress' because it was the first to pass a billion-dollar
budget. The Dependent Pension Bill was passed on December 3, 1889,
providing benefits to Union veterans and their families. The 51st Congress
also approved naval expansion These costly actions earned the fifty-first
presidential administration the name of the "Billion Dollar Congress". The
laws passed during Benjamin Harrison's term in office cost the United
States government over a billion dollars.

154. *Billion Dollar Congress Fact 1:* The 51st legislature was effective from March 4,
1889, to March 4, 1891, during the first 2 years of the administration of
President Benjamin Harrison. **The Sherman Act was established in 1890 that is
within the time in question.**

155.   Surely Your Honor it will be a miscarriage of justice to
punish a hard-working corporation so that you create a
lavish lifestyle of these when the victims are stretched due
to the pandemic and the withholding of support and funds
or their incompetence and corruption. Surely if the money
is to go to the victims better. But they have a lavish
lifestyle in place. But we are going to cut their plans and let
you see the manipulating and deceiving nature of these.
Doing exactly, what they are accusing Facebook of doing.
Ganging up and grouping like wild dogs to strike again

when the wounds are still fresh. This is the youngest business person we have ever heard of. Yes, he is experienced and making or to have made mistakes in saying, through emails and all kinds. But he is young and achieving what he has achieved at that age can make him say things that can be portraying him as a violator of all things the Sherman's Act stands for. But we have given you another version based on accepted methods in business. The Sherman Act is just a tariff collection Act that tricks people. Hard-working people stealing their money. In support, I quote the following to highlight the real reasons behind this Act.

156. Other important laws were passed due to **economic pressures** that included the McKinley tariff, **the Sherman Antitrust Act [Emphasis Added]**, and the Sherman Silver Purchase Act

157. *Billion Dollar Congress Fact 10:* Significance: The extravagant and lavish spending by the Republicans was highly criticized by the public and led to the re-election of the Democratic President, Grover Cleveland, in 1893.

158.   REWARDING THE INABILITY TO DEAL WITH ECONOMIC PRESSURES.

159.   By fining Facebook is not just setting the wrong precedence especially when we all know the reasons behind this Act.

160. Benjamin Harrison and the Congress are portrayed as a "Billion-Dollar Congress," wasting the surplus.

161. Wikipedia.

162.   We will make the law apply to devious, manipulating, and tricking government bodies as well. The court has a duty to move with the times and assess the conditions then and now and come with a sound judgment. Using the law to steal is a crime. We have proved in this case that some laws just because they are still there and not repealed does not mean that they are right or still valid.

TOMORROW'S WORLD ORDER'S PERSPECTIVE

The duty is to you your Honor to order the law as obsolete and not fitting not to Tech giants as well as to modern times. We, therefore, ask the court to disregard the Sherman Act and declare it as a trickery government way of making $billions for doing not. That cannot be allowed. We are the future and we vehemently disagree with this. We are not saying do not take Facebook to court. We are saying that in 1890 no one knew about the digital and tech world. The laws are out of date. Create new fitting laws before you pass judgment. It is up to you. If you fail, then the court will be regarded by us, the new World Leaders, as obsolete too. An institution that needs not only a revamp but breaking up for good before we put a new system of justice. **John Sherman is not going to come today and confess that economic pressures caused them to devise a way of collecting the maximum revenues and tariffs but also that all on trickery grounds to fund a lavish lifestyle when the majority were suffering.** We can hold the court to account. It is up to us to determine our future. This is a miscarriage of justice. Any judgment is flawed and will not stand based on the Sherman Act.

163. B. divestiture of assets, divestiture or reconstruction of businesses (including, but not limited to, Instagram and/or WhatsApp), and such other relief sufficient to restore the competition that would exist absent the conduct alleged in the Complaint, including, to the extent reasonably necessary, the provision of ongoing support or services from Facebook to one or more viable and independent business(es); C. any other equitable relief necessary to restore competition and remedy the harm to competition caused by Facebook's anticompetitive conduct described above; D. a prior notice and prior approval obligation for future mergers and acquisitions; 51 E. that Facebook is permanently enjoined from imposing anticompetitive conditions on access to APIs and data; F. that Facebook is permanently enjoined from engaging in the unlawful conduct described herein; G. that Facebook is permanently enjoined from engaging in similar or related conduct in the future; H. a requirement to file periodic compliance reports with the FTC, and to submit to such reporting and monitoring obligations as may be reasonable and appropriate; and I. any other equitable relief, including, but not limited to,

divestiture or restructuring, as the Court finds necessary to redress and prevent recurrence of Facebook's violations of law, as alleged herein.

164.   THE LAWSUIT IS THERE ONLY TO CREATE A BILLION-DOLLAR FTC AND ITS INTERSTATE SOMETHING WE CAN ONLY ASSOCIATE WITH MAGIC AND WISHFUL THINKING.

165.   A lot has happened then. They used fear to control and dominate the people using fears of slavery to recreate the conditions that will enable them to easily steal from the corporation. That supports my arguments also that they recreated the slavery conditions but using secret digital technology to scare people again so there is a general feeling of anti-trusting of these corporations especially Facebook that deals with data so personal to the people. It worked before when Facebook tried to allow other competitors and be fair according to the Sherman Act the act in question. But end up breached privacy. You can easily see that it is a thin line between protecting people's privacy and avoiding anti-competitive tactics. Now you can see why it is difficult to strike the correct balance.

166.   That supports my argument that the Sherman Act was devised to poke someone in the eye or face. When that person covered the eye, the FTC would poke him or her in his or her private parts and when that person covers the groin area then pokes again in the eye. The person cannot cover both parts of the body at the same time with both hands. That means being stretched. This is why the FTC is so sure would rule in their favor. But this is trickery and not a law. Listen to us Tomorrow's World Order and do what is right for everyone; corporations the FTC, us, and our future kids.

167.   I want the court to note that the same agencies FCT etc. extracted money as fines namely $5 billion. First

accusing the CEO of uncompetitive behavior so that he opens the platform that was once secure. To become competitive as asked. Then come and haunt him with privacy issues. Now he has closed the loophole so now they are on the competitive aspect so that he opens again so that they hit Facebook with another privacy breach lawsuit.

168.   **We are against abuse by corporations but doing it this way is a trick, and this is not justice. THIS IS NOT LAW AND CANNOT STAND BECAUSE IT IS FLAWED.** We stand for the privacy of the people over the competition given the arguments above. Also, because they know that the competition is nonexistent in his market, this is not Standard oil's case. All startups are to complement his firm therefore the talk of competition is flawed. The fact that ten years have passed without another real competitor means all this talk about competition in this way is skewed and cannot stand. They must give the court evidence of a competitor in the USA who could not enter and compete with the potential to do so but failed because of Facebook's acts etc. Facebook CEO explained that it is difficult FOR ANYONE TO ENTER AND CHALLENGE SUCH A POSITION SIMPLY BECAUSE OF THE NATURE OF THE MARKET AND TECHNOLOGY.

TOMORROW'S WORLD ORDER'S PERSPECTIVE

II.

ANTITRUST LAWS
The Case of Facebook V FTC
Tomorrow's World Order's Perspective.

GENERAL VIEWS AT THE TIME.

The people at the time of the enactment of the Sherman Act in 1890 were very skeptical about Trusts which were huge corporations that joined to influence market prices and the competition. The people were concerned, sacred, and untrusting of big corporations. This is in line with the perception of what these big corporations can do and their role in the slave trade. The people of the day saw a threat in the form of Trusts in terms of what they can do as compared to the government and this triggered the new use of Federal government power to control and limit the growth of these Trusts.

CONDITIONS IN 1890 JUST BEFORE THE ENACTMENT OF THE SHERMAN ACT.

The trusts had been involved in slavery and that resulted in deep feelings of mistrust. The people had just got rid of all forms of slavery. The growth of the Trust increased the fears that another form of takeover and slavery was going to happen. The authorities of the day did not want to take any chances so devised a way to control these Trusts and break them before they gathered momentum to become real threats.

DIRECT AND HIDDEN MOTIVES BEHIND THE SHERMAN ACT.

Need to implement and or raise tariffs.

The need to increase Federal spending.

The need to introduce a Protective tariff.

The sheer realization that the corporations and or the Trusts had grown so much to outpace the government triggered a new form of power that was needed to control these. There was the need to control the power of the Trusts and prevent another slave trade situation where people would lose their life, liberty, property rights, and freedoms to these huge corporations directly and indirectly where they control all aspects of life. General mistrust feelings about power, slavery, and good governance.

THE PROBLEM AT HAND.

The antitrust laws were enacted to break the centralization of economies and power from one central place and encourage decentralization. So, no matter what. These laws were there to fight and break any form of centralization as part of their key aims. Hence from outright, they were there to break huge firms and discourage centralization as part of their goal. No matter what you do they will always find a way to block, break, and do away with any form of centralization and or mergers often believed to be associated with multinational companies once associated with slavery. So, a flawed obsolete system that is there to maintain the status quo, regardless. So, no fit for purpose in this economic and political environment. Analysis of efficiencies that are merger-specific is probability-based rather than based on certainties. There is no standardization regarding the evidence required to prove efficiencies brought about by mergers. There is a general hostility to mergers among the agencies, the Federal Bureau of Competition, and the courts. The general belief that the law does not allow efficient defenses. Most of the cost savings and efficiency are often regarded as non-cognizable. Efficiency projections are viewed with skepticism. Even though the onus to present evidence of efficiency is on the merging firms. The need for secrecy can result in vague, incomplete proof presented leaving the courts or agencies concerned with no option but to dismiss efficiency as a defense for a merger. Even though they might have justifiable grounds.

MISUNDERSTANDINGS OF THE IMPORTANT ROLE OF ECONOMIES OF SCALE.

Evidence of efficiencies is often mistrusted as it is probabilistic and often the presented evidence is regarded as ambiguous, non-merger specific, speculative, or unverifiable resulting in most of it rejected as proof. There is a general skepticism regarding the importance of the economies of scale defined as "cost advantages gained by companies when production becomes efficient," Investopedia Dictionary. These arise due to mergers as production is increased spreading the cost over many products and services. Size matters. This is a fact here. The bigger the size the more savings and the more efficient the company becomes. To increase the cost savings and competitive advantage the company must grow fast. The only way is through mergers. Once the companies have merged only, will it be able to realize the cost-saving benefits and in turn, be able to lower prices so that consumers benefit as well? But the problem here is the protectionism aspect that often blocks the move to the stage where the two companies about to merge can merge and create economies of scale. Instead of the merged corporation advancing to the virtuous cycle stage, it remains in the same stage ending up going through a vicious cycle.

VICIOUS CYCLE VERSUS VIRTUOUS CYCLE.

The current system is based on the pyramid system. Often regarded as the strongest and viable system ever made by man. It might have worked but what they do not tell you is that it has features that restrict what would happen naturally. Things that would make it crash and render it obsolete. These things are checks or regulatory measures designed to make the entire system follow a certain predictable path. This causes the system to have a vicious cycle. A path that follows a certain route until it reaches a certain point which is marked as undesirable. This trigger checks into play leading to the implementation of the regulatory burden mechanism to cause it to roll-back just before it crashes as to begin again and repeat the cycle. The following are the stages of company formation and road to growth. Initially, companies have limited incentives to invest. Most companies are there to make a profit just to remain in business. Many players. Many small companies competitively operate in the market. Any increase in profits triggers other small companies to enter the market until everyone else makes profits just to remain in business. Please note this is the idea held by the law implementers when they enacted the Clayton Act and the Sherman Act. Many players are competitively active. Mainly involved in agricultural products. Ideally a group of small farmers etc. There is no centralization of power and influence. Everything is decentralized. This is the perfect market. An ideal world.

LOW-QUALITY PRODUCTS AND SERVICES.

Services and goods are of a low quality which further pushes prices down as competition increases but among smaller companies. One of the companies etc. must outsmart others to dominate and maintain a market share big enough to generate more profits. An incentive to invest further. This can lead to other small companies going out of the business as barriers increase.

COMPLEX PROCEDURES.

If one company succeeds. The large market share attained means extra profits and money to invest. The company then employs complex procedures to create a gap between itself and others. This is a survival tactic. This is now the critical stage. To move out of the vicious cycle, the company must grow to take advantage of the economies of scale. It must keep outsmarting other companies or merge with the others to cut costs through realized efficiencies and economies of scale. This is the critical stage for it. A do or breakpoint. A stage that determines if the vicious cycle is repeated or if the company moves to the next stage of development. The virtuous stage.

REGULATORY BURDEN AS AN OBSTACLE AND THE CURRENT SYSTEM.

The antitrust are laws designed to break up the centralization of power and resources into one huge Trust. I explained below issues related to the trauma and fears associated with Trusts and slavery at the time the laws were enacted in 1890. This has little to do with the competition but more with tariff collection and Federal spending. Decentralization was the key focus. Regulatory burden dictated whether a company would make it or not. Mergers were and are quick ways out of the vicious cycle, but the antitrust laws often come into effect here to break the mergers and roll back everything. This triggers the vicious cycle as the company is left to try again.

LACK OF MARKET FORCES.

The antitrust laws strip the perfect opportunity for a company to cross the bridge to the next stage of development. The regulations make it expensive to run a company that more often lacks funds and incentives to invest. It must start again until another way or opportunity arises.

III.

OUR VIEW OF THE SITUATION AND THE ROAD TO THE VIRTUOUS CYCLE.

We as Tomorrow's World Order; are against obstructive regulations because we know they are simply there to keep the status quo. To keep the pyramid system in place. A system that is obsolete but with checks like the antitrust laws to hold it in place. We also know that it centers around a dictator or monarch. One hidden secretly deep inside it. One who secretly controls and dictates the course of events. One who forbids growth because growth changes the status quo. But the world today is different from the time these laws were enacted. We have corporations accounting for as much as 70% of the top world economies. Their powers and influence are forever growing. Today's agencies, the Federal Trade Commission, and governments use the antitrust laws to control and block these Trusts or corporations out of sheer fear of the unknown. Simply because they have grown to unprecedented levels. We believe so too and have identified a vacuum that needs filling. We must not be afraid of the Trusts and corporations. Instead, we must create an even bigger force to match these as they grow. We as Tomorrow's World Order; are against inferior thinking whereby the antitrust obsolete laws are used to block the inevitable. Instead of blocking these we simply created Tomorrow's World Order to provide a platform to deal with the changing economic environment as well. Look what happened in 1890. When they realized that the Trusts had grown to huge sizes and surpassed the government, they created laws and chose a different body to control them. This body is the Federal Commission working with the Department of Justice. Likewise, we have created Tomorrow's World Order to deal with these. We have things in place too, but we removed the regulatory burden. Instead, we introduced the Facilitation aspect of the system.

FACILITATION.

Too much protection in the form of antitrust laws can be harmful to Trusts. The arguments put forward about the need to 'restore competition so that innovation and free competition can thrive' is just fanciful thinking. The main reason being to maintain the status quo where there are many small businesses but ones who sell poor quality goods. But all make an only profit to remain in business but without any incentives to invest. Yes, it looks like the perfect free market. But we are talking about the first stage of development here where there are no extra profits. No economies of scale. Prices are often high. The products are of mediocre quality. Prices may be lower, but this is in line with the poor product quality as well. The thing all you must know is the fact that this stage is the most sought stage by the agencies, the Federal, and the government. The ideal stage for them. Ask yourself why? To them, they can collect huge tariffs, rents, and taxes. They can offer development incentive related packages. The sums would add up as they can justify funding these. But all these benefits only them. We see this as harm to the consumers rather than benefits in terms of competition. Variety of goods and services, etc. Yes, it looks like the ideal world to them because office spaces are all occupied. Company buildings are all fully occupied. Tariffs collected are huge which justifies, in turn, huge federal spending as well. Everyone has a job. They only wait to break a merger to roll back the situation and start all over again at the expense of the people through high tariffs, taxes, rents, etc. We as the new global leaders believe that facilitation is the key. We are stuck in the defensive stages of development. To go to another stage of development. We must embrace change. We must facilitate growth. We must be patient as well. Not be too judgmental. These companies are going through new virgin roads. It is a learning curve. They can make mistakes. So be patient. Facilitate as you can. Ban antitrust laws. Instead, encourage growth even at the expense of competition because the stage where there is competition only indicates an immature level of development. When there is technological advancement monopoly is part of the system. This is central to our existence. Everything has a leader. Antitrust laws are against that notion. They require many peers all at the same level. But a house has a head. A school has a headteacher. A country has a president. A military has Chief-in-command the world must have a leader. Hence us Tomorrow's World Order. So as a market must have a market leader. One to use economies of scale to trickle back the benefits through reduced prices of high-quality goods. This is different from the stages the antitrust laws will leave. Although there is competition and variety, etc. the products are often of low quality anywhere. Who would pay more for mediocre quality when there are quality goods possibly at lower prices? We have global issues because the system is obsolete and does not fit the changing environment. So, we facilitate mergers. Encourage these to grow without the regulatory burden but we can put monitoring agencies to see if there are not increasing prices when they should be lowering prices. We can aim to eliminate the harm to consumers. We can address deliberate violations that involve gaining unfavorable at the expense of the consumers. We are a global phenomenon and are not afraid of Trusts. We believe now that the governments, the interstate, and the

TOMORROW'S WORLD ORDER'S PERSPECTIVE

Federal Trade Commission are the ones acting to harm the consumers.

LAWS AGAINST THE GOVERNMENT, THE INTERSTATE, AND THE FEDERAL TRADE COMMISSION, ETC.

We would rather penalize the above for harming the people. First, we can argue that the laws are for their benefit at the expense of the consumers. More competition for lower quality services will harm than do good. Most are doing this to have a job and stay on the payroll. Most corporations follow the company's laws that are fair and anti-discriminatory. That places the burden on corporations to do more for their employees. Corporations are doing jobs supposed to be done by governments etc. Providing health insurance, building low-cost housing, addressing most of the issues that in the long run they do better than harm the people. Whereas the interstates and governments are ripping off, the people using sophisticated technology to maximize say tariff collections. See more details below. Our laws will now drag these to court instead of corporations. But I am not saying that all corporations are angels. Where privacy violations or unfair competition practices are identified we can deal also with the corporations. But care must be exercised as they are entering uncharted virgin waters. They can come across new things. But compensating the very people affected must be a new way forward rather than for the corporation to be asked to donate to a charity or give to the government institutions, etc. The affected people must benefit from the violation as the corporation is found guilty or not. The onus is placed on corporations to address any violations with compensation. Laws against the government's use of secret modern-day slavery to control, dictate, and steal from the consumers, etc.

TOMORROW'S WORLD ORDER'S PERSPECTIVE

THE SHIFT IN EMPHASIS FROM THE REGULATORY BURDEN TO FACILITATION THEN TO A NEW ADVANCED STAGE OF DEVELOPMENT WHERE THERE ARE TANGIBLE BENEFITS.

The current system places emphasis on competition, lower prices, and more choices, etc. but with overall mediocre benefits. We have been stuck in this stage for over seventy years. We believe there is a lot more we can do. Competition for the sake of competition is meaningless. Instead, let growth be natural so that in the end we realize the full benefits of reduced prices of high-quality goods and services. Naturally, corporations will take over from governments by providing all the services governments are supposed to provide. But we are there to make sure that they play fair. No government or Federal agencies will be able to fully understand these things. Then regulate at the same time. Then think ahead as to see all humanity in a new stage of development where there is abundant wealth for everyone. Only we can help humanity have the best of both worlds. The huge corporations and the regulatory bodies namely, governments, FTC, and other agencies. They cannot aim to provide what is best for everyone. The consumers and the corporations at the same time and try to maximize say tariff collection.

IV.

THE RIGHT OF CORPORATIONS TO USE THE SWOT ANALYSIS.

SWOT analysis is short for Strength, Weaknesses, Opportunities, and Threats. The SWOT analysis is a survival and growth tool for all businesses. A tool used to set oneself above the rest. This is a survival technique which corporations can use to analyze their strength and act accordingly. Then look at their weaknesses and then find ways to strengthen themselves. They look at opportunities as well. Can mergers bring us economies of scale? They might ask. If yes which way is best to go about it. What are the threats? Once identified the threats must be acted upon. There is no point to do a SWOT analysis and when you have identified your threats. Then do nothing about them. Managers go to universities to learn these skills because these are the only tactics that will see them grow to start making real profits and gain a huge market share. You must outsmart your opponents. Find that competitive edge to do it. So, accusations of anticompetitive strategies are flawed. I base my remarks on the fact that the SWOT analysis tool is a lawful skill taught at the university. Approved by the company's act as lawful. Using it is part of everything business-wise. Corporations are guided by the company's laws. It can be predatory but still within the law. Using this tool is the only way you could achieve growth if the strategy adopted does not justify illegality. This is not like where governments hack everyone medically then secretly steals their ideas as they spy on them through video senders that twin your computer or phone screens with theirs. Hacking their computers or phones, etc. to monitor what they are doing then steal and sell their ideas, etc. In return offer them the so-called protection. Where they start telling everyone that they are guiding that person under the support packages, etc. But selling their ideas behind their backs in return for donations, etc. This is what is illegal. What Facebook, etc. is doing by acquiring smaller businesses is within the business model. First, the company is selling to Facebook because they find the deal lucrative. That means Facebook is going by the company laws that must precede these antitrust laws. Instagram's business model says sell when the offer is right. Instagram's business model says the same. They sold the companies to Facebook willingly because the price was lucrative and not at gunpoint.

ANTICOMPETITIVE ALLEGATIONS FLAWED FROM OUTSET. AS SMALL COMPANIES WERE CREATED TO BE SOLD AT A PROFIT TO FACEBOOK ANYWHERE.

Most of these small companies create a business model intending to sell it to say Facebook. This is the reason for starting a business. They got into the business so that they can sell to Facebook. In company laws, there are startups to do just that. Start a business to sell it to a giant at that time. Once the time has arrived. The job is done. Most start-ups pass it to a big tech giant at a lucrative price so that they go into other areas. So, if all the small businesses have the same business model. Get it to create a great idea that has the tech giant at heart. Create the business and make it attractive that Facebook will come asking for it. When they do. Sell quickly. Get the money and start another to pass it over at a profit. Then the talk of anticompetitive behavior is flawed. That was the aim of the small business anywhere so how can that be anticompetitive if the company was created for Facebook to acquire it. Any other company if put in that position would do the same. This is not specific to Facebook, but a taught way to get a competitive edge. It is part of a taught and approved management system called SWOT analysis. Hence the more cases of anti-competitive behavior, etc. They are in business to use all these tools to get that edge over others to gain a huge market share.

The fact that they are registered under the company's act means you have no right to regulate this area if they are within the law. Where there is no illegality. Protectionism is associated with illegality. Originate with the pyramid system with Pharaohs and kings or dictatorship. Outdated practices. It revolves around bribery, unfair practices, regarding sovereign and legal entities as incapable hence in need of handouts and help. Yes, some of these companies fail but they know that before they even start the business. In most cases, the lawsuits are politically motivated. They let the administrative part approve all these mergers with excellence. When things go wrong politically, they then group like wild dogs and bring lawsuits.

FREEDOM OF ACTIONS.

The idea is to encourage growth to extreme levels. The history we have is for regulated worlds. To be honest we have achieved nothing. The problems then are still the problems now. Tomorrow's World Order believes that we are operating below our capacity. We as humans can do better than this. We must be in a different stage of development. This we can only achieve through getting out of our comfort zone. Resist the temptation of sticking to outdated useless institutions and ways of doing things. Surely what was best in 1890 and fit for the Sherman Act can be the same today. Quick thinking and the balls not to be afraid of change is the only way forward.

FIRST, YOU MUST UNDERSTAND THAT THE WHOLE SYSTEM IS BASED ON THE PYRAMID SYSTEM.

What is not to love they all would argue? The pyramid has lasted 3 000 years and still stands to this day.

The only system that would stand the test of time above all. It is durable and strong. Pyramids are ambassadors of longevity. The political, economic, social financial system of any country is all based on the pyramid system. A tried and trusted system that works, that has worked and will continue to work they might argue. But they have missed one point. That it relies on the presence of a Pharaoh or monarchy at the center and slavery or oppression for it to work. But then again there is no slavery. It was abolished years ago so how can you speak of slavery in the 21st century? Ladies and gentlemen after reading this you will notice the fault of the current system. Trust me you will agree with me that the current system is the problem. But first, let me explain. A pyramid even though it has stood the test of time it has drawbacks in that it relies on a huge base of people. Previously a place once for slaves etc. at the base who will hold and support the top. A change in shape means the instability of the pyramid with the resulting consequences of tumbling down. But first before going further let me divert your attention to the pyramid schemes. I know this might seem irrelevant here but please bear with me.

PYRAMID SCHEMES.

Okay, it might sound irrelevant here, but the idea is the same in the long run in that the current system has controls put in place to pace the speed and control the collapse associated with the pyramid if any but most to avoid the collapse. One of these which is critical to the issues at hand is the Roll-back feature. A feature that keeps everything in check and as the collapse is about to happen the

TOMORROW'S WORLD ORDER'S PERSPECTIVE

Rollback function comes into play to take back the system to the beginning where the process is restarted as the cycle begins again. This is what we as the new global leaders are saying is the greatest critical issue at hand. For those who are for the current system, they use this to argue that the system is perfect since it has never collapsed as expected and is still running perfectly. Perfectly?? Are you sure I might ask? Okay to make this clearer picture when you are about to have an orgasm or climax. You are seconds away from that climax period when suddenly someone screams that you lose the tenseness associated with moments before the climax. You go from 100 to zero suddenly. You find out that the scream was probably nothing. You can go back to the point you were just before the scream startled you. You must start again from the start even though now the journey to that climax point might be faster. The scream will have turned everything off. Now you are about to climax or orgasm if female then another shouting outside your bedroom window startled you again. Imagine these disturbances happening throughout without any climax forever? Of course, you will keep trying to go on because you have not reached that critical point. You have even more energy to reach that climax point, so you remain determined. But in fact, you are not going anywhere as the disturbances are meant that you do not climax forever. Imagine never reaching that stage? Okay, you might last longer but without the critical climax point, it might be pointless. Of course, it keeps you going. Now determined to achieve the climax but without any results. Ladies and gentlemen this is what the so-called current system is all about. Yes, to most and the naked eye it seems a perfect system. One that has been there forever and no doubt one that will be there tomorrow but with slight change and benefits at all. Why? This is the only way it can go on forever without collapsing. There are things in place as I mentioned above to hold it from collapsing. Things that prevent the collapse but reverting it to the beginning just as it reached levels deemed critical that if there is no intervention, then the system would collapse. A switch is needed to stop just before the system reaches the critical level so that it reverts to the beginning and starts again. This is what I call the Rollback feature. For if the system is left to proceed the outcome would be a state undesirable as it will mean the change of the system as we know it. Welcome to Tomorrow's World Order. The system we are proposing is diamond-shaped.

V.

OUR DIAMOND-SHAPED SYSTEM VERSUS THE CURRENT SYSTEM OF THE PYRAMID.

Our system is the evolved system one that follows the current pyramid system. The current system as I have relentlessly argued in my main book Tomorrow's World Order is based on a pyramid that relies on a broader base with most of the people below the poverty line. Mind you this system was modeled after the Egyptian system but without slavery and the dictatorship or monarchy at the center something they just say but something still at the center of this system even though now in secrecy. The Egyptians relied on cheap slavery labor and for more people being at the base poor and overworked to support the lavish lifestyles of the pharaohs at the top. This is the basis of the current system. It all boils down to the numbers. The less the numbers below the bottom line the unstable it becomes. Again, I will take you to the pyramid scheme. People at the bottom join through the collected taxes they pay and are promised returns in terms of protection by those at the top. But to remain sustainable the numbers must be controlled as protection cannot be awarded to all as it grows but that means at one point the number enrolled would be larger than the protection provided that riots etc. would eventually occur causing the collapse in the form of civil wars. So, the current system has what I will call checks.

CURRENT PYRAMID SYSTEM AND ITS CHECKS TO KEEP IT IN CONTROL AND PLACE.

The main reason why the pyramid system has stood the test of time is the fact that it does not focus on growth but on maintaining the status quo. Any further increase or decrease will impact the stability of the system. So, maintaining the current numbers and activities is paramount. Most systems have met their demise and collapsed because they lack the numbers check-in that they have focused on growth to their demise. In a pyramid system, the state is the main player with greater roles to control everything. This is one of the other checks. The state must have the absolute power to control and govern otherwise if someone else or something else takes over then the system is destined to collapse. This is critical as you will discover later about the lawsuit at the hand of Facebook versus the US state Attorney. A new change was on the horizon at the time the Act was implemented. A new never seen before force of power had just emerged. The growth of a large corporation from the 1870s called Trusts. The adopted pyramid system had never seen power consolidated in Trusts that they outpace the government power. Surely this signaled the need to put checks in place in response to the growth of these Trust. As I will explain later the Trust were threats to the existence of the states, they operated as they threatened the fabric of the existence of the current system. The Act arose to limit and control the threats posed by the Trust to ensure the survival of the system. The Trust were threats to the future of the states and the current system in several ways.

One.

They changed the makeup of the system. Their presence meant fewer individuals' small companies that meant less collection of tariffs and taxes.

Two.

That meant less state and federal spending as the small companies will be put out of business. That would also mean rising living standards meaning fewer people below the poverty line. That would mean an unstable system that is posed to collapse unless a match of cutting the numbers in the above level is achieved as well.

Three.

At the time fears of what big corporations can do were among the people after witnessing what power and slavery can do. People were so determined to make sure that these big corporations would never be so big to implement slavery again directly or indirectly.

Four.

The implication of the role of these Trusts is seen as putting the government out of business. Recall I argued that the system is based and relies on the idea of the government taking center stage. The government must be seen to take the center role. The government must be the main player. The sole provider of roads, houses, social services, etc. But that all changed with the rise of these trusts. They took over as they had enough money to buy out governments and build new cities, etc. That was a threat to the current system that something had to be done or else the system was heading for collapse. But the government had been ruled out to match these. The only way to deal with these was to implement the same checks as in the system. The same checks that had meant the existence and longevity of the system. Systems of controls and monitoring with the aim to Rollback the corporations to manageable sizes before they become so big to crash the system. So, from the outset, the aim is to maintain the status quo. Like they argue why not? This is after all the longest and best system known to humankind. All they had to do was to control growth. Everything can grow to a certain size before the checks come into play. Breaking everything and Rolling Back everything to the known good times. If the system can go through these checks so as the Trusts. Hence the introduction of the Sherman

Act. You must understand that it hints at the competition but the idea behind this Act is the raising of Tariffs. It is a pyramid after all. It relies on numbers at the base being many be it small companies, etc. for tariffs, etc. The state where the Trusts operate can charge and collect tariffs and rents for many companies and cannot collect the same amount from just one big corporation. Say they can collect $50 from 100 small companies. But if the Trust has sent the other companies out of business, the state can collect just $50 from the Trust that has consolidated the small companies or sent others out of the business. Small companies in numbers can mean rent and a lot of offices occupied justify the state implementing growth packages, but this is a different situation if it is only one big Trust. But to understand the implications of this first we theoretically assess what we as Tomorrow's World Order believe will happen if the checks were not in place and mind you this Sherman Act is one of the checks to control and maintain the status core. We as the new leaders believe that the current system is obsolete. This is because it is based on fanciful unrealistic views of the world we live in. That could explain the chaos you are all in with economic and financial crush and problems. We believe that this trick of putting checks in place is not just dangerous but stupid as well. I argued that the current system collapsed decades ago. Wars were signals to humanity to change and move to the next stage of development. Refer to Tomorrow's World Order about the stages of development we have postulated. But here I will point out that if nature is left to take control no matter how unappealing the next stages will be in the end; it will turn out perfect.

OUR SYSTEM THE DIAMOND SHAPE VERSUS THE CURRENT PYRAMID.
We believe that if the system is not controlled with checks like the

TOMORROW'S WORLD ORDER'S PERSPECTIVE

Sherman Act that tricks people to think that it acts in the interest of companies. The current pyramid will be turned into a diamond naturally. Yes, they will be a collapse. But the collapse of the already collapsed obsolete pyramid system that had dictatorship, slavery, and oppression at the center of it. Only the Trust and big corporations will take the people out of the poverty line. Lifting everyone off the ground that the broad base of the pyramid will end up an inverted pyramid meaning spinning half revolution that is one hundred and eighty degrees. That the narrow once top becomes the base and at the top other shapes began to form. Yes, there must be the collapse of the current system first to take the people out of the poverty line. This is because big corporations or Trusts will have enough money to provide services and accommodations fast and provide incomes to lift the people out of poverty. Something which the government cannot and will never do simply because the government is a tricking bastard. In that, it takes people's incomes with its huge left hand and gives the people in terms of $5 handout meaning useless handouts so that forever people will remain below the poverty line. The main reason being that they want to maintain the status quo. Any change at the bottom will topple the top level to the top. The level at the top says the hospitals and ambulances or the police depend on many homeless and people on drugs etc. to justify the large top-level numbers. Remove all homeless and drug addicts and they will end up running out of work. The current hostility towards large corporations is not like the time of the Sherman Act where fears of being enslaved somehow were raised. This is the 21st century even though secret slavery exist I would argue that the fears now are imaginary as compared to the time of the Act. Mistrust of these large corporations was real even perceived fears ended up real as the slavery trauma was still in the people's minds. Now it is a survival strategy by the government and all its state in that allowing these big corporations will only result in their collapse. Remove all the checks especially the Roll-back one and see the collapse of the system. The system as I have argued collapsed decades ago. The only thing holding it in place are these checks. Imagine a fuse that blows off rendering the circuit not working. Now an electrician comes and instead of replacing the fuse with a better one that is more powerful or resistant to the increasing voltage. The electrician uses a wire instead to connect the two points. Yes, the wire will work but also it is a matter of time before something goes wrong. The more the current increases over time the more it will create a time bomb in the future. Instead of letting the growth come naturally the government and states will put checks to destroying and rollback anything that will pass the acceptable size. But now imagine where the pyramid will turn a half revolution upside down lifting all those below the bottom line up and probably toppling the once few privileged elites at the top? A process destined to happen. A process that will invert or flip vertically the pyramid as the once top now becomes the below few.

VI.

THE ONLY WAY FORWARD. NO CHECKS AND CONTROLS.

I argued in my main book Tomorrow's World Order that we are in the defensive stage of development. A stage where fears stop humanity from advancing to other stages. A stage where imaginary or real fears cause humankind to be stuck in this stage. The fear of memory from past trauma e.g., from slavery makes people put checks in place to make sure that this will never happen again. Checks to keep the status quo simply because this is the stage people know and trust. Anything else and any change falls into what they call the Antitrust. Not to be confused with the name given to the huge corporations. The antitrust are things if left alone will lead to the change in the status quo. These things need checks to be put in place either to control and monitor them then act to Rollback to a manageable less level of threat. These activities act and things are regarded as threats to the status quo therefore the existence of the system. So, the government will be put out of business if they stick to this obsolete pyramid system. Ok, the system has stood the stand of time, but we are still stuck in the defensive stage of development. If the current system is in place, the problems seventy-five years ago will remain the problems of the future. To move to the next stage of development major changes must take place. At one point a new ruler must be in place one above a government. One above the Federal state. Welcome to Tomorrow's World Order. I will explain why. The Sherman Act arose out of the sheer realization that the government had been beaten in terms of power, money, and control.

TOMORROW'S WORLD ORDER'S PERSPECTIVE

The Trusts had become so huge that the government had no power at all against these corporations as slowly they took over from the government. Building houses for its workers, building roads, providing services and wages and medical services for its employees meaning to thousands of people. Roles that must be part of the government if the current system is to be sustained. So, the Sherman act introduced a power strong enough to match at least or do something about these Trusts in the form of the Federal Committee with powers to show the Trusts who is the boss by breaking all these. Now the Trusts we have today, have grown even much stronger and powerful than the time of the implementation of the Sherman Act but now there are new raised fears. Who now will be able to deal with these Trusts or new corporations like Facebook, Amazon, Google, etc.? Their wealth has meant that in the future they will become uncontrollable. The problems are mainly the issues that they will become real threats. If for example, say they become political. The huge vast amount of wealth and the number of people working for them will mean outpacing not just the government in terms of power but also the Federal law and Committee. Now there are new fears just as at the time of the Sherman Act but now the fears are about the even more threat of these corporations that the current system has no clues what they will do with corporations like Facebook that they are left to fight all of them ganging up on them to put injunctions to break them up before things get out of hand. I will point out that Facebook has become the greatest power threat as it now influences the political voting system as people can now advertise only through its channels, therefore, have an impact to influence the outcome. Making the political system predictable to some extent.

TOMORROW'S WORLD ORDER'S PERSPECTIVE

TOMORROW'S WORLD ORDER AS THE ANSWER TO FACEBOOK AND OTHER COMPANIES' GROWTH AND THREATS.

It is a fact that during the Sherman Acts implementation into law the trusts were power-hungry and mad corporations. Now picture today's corporations like Facebook and its influence or potential influence in the political system surely the fear is real. But most of the governments and states are now on their knees compounded by the pandemic that they are now wishing for real change has failed for the past seventy-five years since the end of the Second World Order. But change can also mean their end as they depend on the checks like these Antitrust laws and removing these and letting nature take a toll will mean their collapse as the Trusts or corporations are destined to put them out of business. A rapid removal of current checks will see corporations take over all government functions and improve the lives of the people bring real value to the lives of the people. They will be able to do all which the governments are failing to do. They would bring democracy as they are run under the company's laws that are more democratic and fairer than the government system builds on trickery and master-slave relationship. When this happens even the Federal laws will be out of touch as all checks will have been removed. This is because to grow and take humanity out of the defensive stages. A lot of things. All unfavorable to the government and the current system must happen.

   a) The current system will eventually collapse.
   b) The current legal system that is prohibitive will die out and unless governments reform and stand for instead of against bigger corporations and trusts, they have no place. This is because people will see them for who they are. Manipulating and tricking bastards asking homeless people to provide jobs for them. Keeping the people below the poverty line deliberately so they have jobs. That alone will make people

trust the once not trusted Trust and corporations turning away from governments that they will up rise and revolt against governments that the trust and corporations to protect their interests in terms of the welfare of their employees will turn political as they will end up seeing the need to control order as well.

c) This means that a new, even powerful player must be in place to control and oversee the trust and corporations. This is the natural way of evolution and the only way things will end up being.

d) The corporations and the Trusts will end up revolting and finding ways to challenge and win against the Antitrust laws. This is because their growth and power will in the end mean finding ways to beat the government at its games. How? I believe if it is possible to sue the government using the reverse antitrust laws.

e) Reversal use of antitrust laws. I think the corporations and Trust can use the reverse arguments the Federal Committee uses against them to launch lawsuits against them as well. This is because they all do the same. Grouping and filing lawsuits against these corporations just like the corporations and Trusts do as they gather to determine the price to sell a product at. So, it will be possible for corporations to launch anti-discriminatory laws in that these interstates are not acting for the public good of the people. I will look at this issue in recommendations and the way forward. But here the corporations will need only to prove that the interstate is acting against what is good for the public. The corporations will only need to prove that they have taken over what is supposed to be the interstate's duties rendering them obsolete and therefore not in a capacity to challenge them. This is because they will have improved people's lives. They will have taken the people out of the poverty zone. They need to provide that these Antitrust are based on skewed fears.

TOMORROW'S WORLD ORDER'S PERSPECTIVE

This is because the current trusts and corporations have changed. They are no longer involved with all abolished evil practices like slavery that triggered the Sherman Act. They need to prove that interstate's fears are regarding the tariffs they collect. Something that negatively impacts people. The fact that the corporations and Trust are improving the lives of these people and the government on the other hand is stealing money from these people through taxes will make the antitrust laws obsolete.

f) More critical to this book is the fact that the governments and interstate themselves have taken the roles the trust used to do that triggered the Sherman Act. It can now be argued that the government themselves are the ones now involved in the secret modern slavery rather than the corporations. I will explain in detail below.

VII.

GOVERNMENTS AS THE MASTER MINDERS AND VEHICLES OF
MODERN-DAY SECRET SLAVERY AND OPPRESSION OF THEIR PEOPLE.
THEY HAVE BECOME ANTI MANKIND.

It is a fact that like I argued that the current system is based on a pyramid from the Egyptian system of 3000 BC a system that has been refined over decades and centuries getting new meaning after the Second World War. The system is based on a dictatorship of some king and control of everything is paramount to maintain the system. The need to control the people has meant the governments taking over the once evil Trust and corporations and doing the very things they are denouncing as evil but now secretly and underground. Undetected using sophisticated technology to human hack everyone in the name of medical records and now in the need to control the people. That has meant hacking people and secretly using drone technology and miniature airplane parts; GPS, black boxes, medical diodes, and electromagnetic nerve tampering to recreate slavery condition. To control the people in terms of who dies and when they die. Who works and where? Who pays bills and when? They have taken over controlling every aspect of life. Using all these to collect tariffs and determining who rents what and when. The governments have become anti-humans hacking people with radiation-emitting gadgets to maximize tariff collection as they can say for example pinpoint where someone is and parked say a car then send their parking fees collection agents to hit that driver relentlessly with fines. A form of cheating therefore has become anti-people. This means they have become and caused real harm to the people they are supposed to protect.

TOMORROW'S WORLD ORDER'S PERSPECTIVE

I believe charges of hostage-taking can succeed against all governments and interstate who have to hold everyone at ransom as hostages as they illegally mostly at birth or try to use the pandemic to hack and justify illegal hacking practices where they use say torture to zone people in certain areas, etc. to influence occupants' rates and viability of the area, etc.

The benefits to the people by these interstates and governments in recent years have become minimal. Companies like Amazon are providing cheaper housing for the people. They are improving the lives of the people by giving employees shares as well as lifting everyone out of the poverty zone. Now the antitrust attacks against big corporations are with malicious intentions simply because the corporations are taking them out of the business. Big corporations have become more people-centered than interstate and governments.

The Trust and corporations can argue that the interstates are discriminating against them ganging upon them when all the attacks are concerning tariffs, something which harms the people. Big corporations will mean fewer revenues and empty office and company space. They can argue that the pandemic has hit the interstates and governments hard and all this talk about anti-competitive of say Facebook is just a cover to their filling pinched in the pocket. Hence motive will harm the already suffering people.

Corporations can now argue that the interstate, the Federal Committee, etc. are now unprepared to deal with the changing economic, social, and financial environment in that they have been rendered incapable of doing anything for the people without further harming them. The pandemic and growth of these corporations have meant less importance of these interstates, federal, and the government other than being frustrations of progress and development. The pandemic will render them incapable of dealing with and representing the people.

They can also argue that their size and growth and their acts in improving humankind and living standards make them part and parcel of life now that they have become mandatory and must keep growing to provide full benefits to the people. The calls to break up these corporations and trust is personal other than anything else to the interstate, Federal, and governments concerned in that for them it is a survival issue rather than a looking after the people and ensuring effective competition. It has everything to do with the reduced tariff revenues, something that used to harm the already strained people.

THE ISSUE OF ROLLBACK IS COUNTERPRODUCTIVE. THE ISSUE OF THE VICIOUS CYCLE.

The calls to break up, monitor, and ask for injunctions and other forms of control are short-sighted calls that will keep and maintain the status quo but keep most of the people below the poverty line. I explained why the calls are made.

The idea behind and business is to grow and become not just profitable but be able to reduce cost due to economies of scale. In the end, the consumer will benefit greatly from reduced prices and a better value of goods. Growth is associated also with improved wages, better health cover for the lucky employees, and the trickling down effect. That the cities with these huge corporations, etc. gain a lot from increased disposable incomes. Meaning these corporations might be doing good rather than harm.

The system itself depends on the Roll Back feature to remain intact for without this feature it will collapse. The antitrust act as argued above is one of the checks in place to make sure that the corporations and trust will not grow to uncontrollable sizes. The fear is in the fact that it will be hard to control these companies rather than their impact on competition, etc. The more they grow the bigger they become and the more powerful they will become. The other crucial factor is or was the lack of a global leader. One higher than the federal Committee of any country. A real global overseer and leader not just to control these corporations as they grow but to direct everyone on how to go about it. Now Tomorrow's World Order has seen the crucial gap and anticipated the problems and challenges ahead and rose. We are the solution to these growth fears. Surely how can these corporations be harmful to the people? This is the way life is intended and the only way to a new stage of development. The road to the Diamond shape system with a pointed narrow base and everyone else above the poverty line.

So far, I think you can guess that our stance regarding the Antitrust laws is that they are obsolete. They have run the course of their time and must be shelved. In my book Tomorrow's World Order, I argued that these laws must be viewed in line with circumstances and political, social, economic environment at the time as compared to now. To us, they are a pain. The governments today are the ones doing more harm to their people. We have proof beyond doubt that the governments since the abolishing of say slavery have poured billions into technology that does the abolished acts remotely operated like drones and using GPS technology to steal from the already strained people. The launching of the Facebook case is in response to the fewer revenues they are getting especially concerning the effects of the pandemic. Secondly the political implication of social media in politics. This is the real reason behind Facebook's lawsuit rather than the reliance upon arguments of "to restore competition so that innovation and free competition thrive,". Facebook has become a powerhouse enough to influence politics. But all this is also the people's choice. No one is forced: correctly, to use Facebook. They choose because it is best for them. The issues of growth and buying out of rivals and consolidating of companies are part and parcel of growth. The moment they issued a company number or license to trade means they indirectly also accepted that the aim is to grow. The issue of asking a company to grow to a certain level is interference with a sovereign company in that a company is an entity if their acts do not bring harm to the people must not be interfered upon. This issue of Rollback is not just contrary to the basis of issuing a license but a breach of the fundamental rights and norms behind running a company.

TOMORROW'S WORLD ORDER'S PERSPECTIVE

The fact that growth and all kinds of problems are still prevalent today with all these checks and antitrust having been there for so long means that these antitrust laws have themselves become against the public good. They are there for the benefits of the interstates, the federal branch, and the government concerned. Honestly, nothing today about all these is beneficial to the people. They are now doing more harm. Manipulating, torturing, and intimidating the people to pay up using tricks and above all themselves involved in acts against all international laws. Human hacking to monitor and influence competition themselves. To abuse and monitor illegal activities. Hacking to increase tariff collection. Copyright violations that they use sophisticated gadgets to hack and steal information using video senders and benefit unfavorably.

VIII.

STEALING AND COPYRIGHT VIOLATIONS BY THE GOVERNMENTS
AND THE INTERSTATE AND THE FEDERALS AS A FACTOR AGAINST
THE ANTITRUST LAWS.

The governments themselves over the years have relied on stolen information from the people through spying using plane technology GPS, the satellite, and video senders to hack the people first then use the hack to steal their ideas and projects they are working on and use radiation to kill them then sell the information for a donation. Now that the people have become clever that in conjunction with the huge corporations like Amazon or Facebook or even Twitter, they have chosen to report to these giants and corporations through self-published material. Most are offering platforms to do everything these interstates, governments, and federals used to offer. Now Facebook and Amazon are offering business startups, loans, finance, advertisements, web pages, etc., and platforms they can write and publish. That means these have all the secrets and videos showing human hacking used to steal information before the government people offer it in return for a donation. We have the hospitals deliberately hacking people, stealing their ideas, and then damaging the brain through rotary propellers and or medical diodes fired into the body to shake the brain of these people then pretend it is them guiding them as part of the so-called evil protection in countries like Britain. This is happening everywhere and the main issue at hand is that these corporations have put them out of business. The people could see real benefits if these corporations are left to grow then provide benefits to the people through economies of scale. Better that way because this is the only long-term solution to all global problems. This takes us back to the issue at the beginning about climax or orgasm. Do you prefer a huge orgasm or several but frustration none climax sessions? This is exactly what is happening with these antitrust laws. They are there to make all these corporations not climax to trickle roll the benefits to the people. In the end, it is costly to run these companies and impossible to pass the benefits. We are the future and from now on we dictate how we will run the world. We stand firm against antitrust laws for the sack of control and regulation. For seventy-five years they have done all they can, but I tell you that the same issues then are the same issues now. We stand firm against control just for the sake of it. Control for the sake of providing jobs. It is like saying keep the homeless people homeless so that the police have jobs. Keep the drug addicts infect torture them first secretly so that they take more drugs to provide the ambulance and hospitals jobs to do. It is like breaking up Facebook so that we have smaller companies that give us competition and lower prices, etc. Yes, they might lower prices but hey wake up this is what has been going on for the past seventy years and we are honestly fed up. This is because this is the wrong approach. You are telling the small companies that grow we will nature you, but you must grow to a certain size but at the same time you yourselves are stealing from the people. Giving with the right hand and taking with the left. We are against Facebook and other corporations only if they impact and harm the people both in the short term and long term.

But caution must be exercised where they might impact the people in the short term to provide long term benefits. We stand for real change. Therefore, we must consider both the impact. It is no argument to declare to break a company just for competition purposes. We as world leaders will monitor say price changes over say a period and assess if the growth of the corporations will have made a difference to the people's lives. We must think ahead and plan. Useless frustrative laws that severely impact overall growth without tangible benefits must be replaced or abandoned.

DOUBLE STANDARDS.

The lawsuits tend to attack Facebook for exactly what they all are doing as well. We need a responsible government that appreciates the help these huge corporations are doing and going to do. We have been stuck in the defensive stage because there is too much use of these restrictive laws most honestly if you understand the way they were introduced is out of date. The interstate all combines and gang up on the huge corporations and do exactly what they are saying is wrong or what they stand for. Most are there to encourage company formations, but they cry foul play when things do not go their way.

IX.

THE POLITICAL ASPECTS OF THESE TRUSTS AND CORPORATIONS.

I know for a fact that the lawsuits arose out of the sheer shock and realization of the impact of giants like Facebook in determining the political route as well and their influence in the social media network. But issues must be with supporting the small companies to grow as big as the market leader then calls for a break. To us, the only thing that can trigger the calls for break up is when the corporations or Facebook in this case is violating the people's rights and going unchallenged repetitively and sustained over a period. A one-time breach can also trigger the calls. It all depends on other factors and the severity of the breach. Most important is what the company does afterward. We have the belief that the road they are taking is uncharted waters in that no one has tried that before growing at such growth and if there is a breach and is not material or intentional. Then that company can be forgiven given that they compensate the victims and do not gain from the breach. But where they have gained unfairly that can trigger calls for a breakup. I think compensation might be the central focus to give the new growth leaders time and opportunities to proceed forward to provide compound benefits at the end. But again, privacy issues must be taken seriously were not accompanied by compensation and redress of the procedures and practices and not to repeat that can trigger the calls. We will look at cases like these about all world events. Imagine a nuclear bomb killing thousands and not even a person held accountable then the loss of data getting people imprisoned? But again, each case must be decided on its merits.

TOMORROW'S WORLD ORDER'S PERSPECTIVE

SELF-CONTRADICTIONS.

The current system like I have argued is based on a pyramid nevertheless with checks to keep it afloat. The state has a key role as the main actor and provider of everything. Responsible for tariffs collection. Maintain competition, etc., and declare that they provide growth and improve lives. When their presence is the very fact that people are in the mess in the first place. It is like shooting themselves in the first place. They say we want you to grow. We can help you grow. But when they have grown, they use the rollback check to start over again. The only way to bring change is for them to pave the way for someone else.

TIME FOR CORPORATIONS AND TRUST TO TAKE A LEADING ROLE.

We believe that for the past seventy years people have trusted the governments to get them out of this mess and I can see that they have failed big time. It is therefore time to give a chance to these corporations and Trusts to take humanity out of the defensive stages to a new stage of development under the guidance of Tomorrow's World Order.

CASE STUDY

FACEBOOK VERSUS THE US ATTORNEY. ANTITRUST LAWSUIT.

The allegations.
Facebook has been accused of:
Abusing its dominance in the digital market. Using its power unfairly to squash or hindered potential threats.
To have engaged in anticompetitive behavior
To have entrenched and maintained its monopoly denying the consumers the benefit of competition.
Therefore because of this must be broken up. The Federal Trade Commission: The Bureau of competition is seeking a permanent injunction in court. The effect of this is to request that Facebook divert assets. Referring to Instagram and WhatsApp.

The lawsuit requires Facebook also to notify the state officials of any future mergers worth more than $10 million.

The lawsuit aims to roll back Facebook's anticompetitive conduct. Then restore competition to make free competition and innovation thrive.

The lawsuit accused Facebook of neutralizing competitive threats by gobbling them up.

Facebook is also accused of opening its doors to third parties to use its platform for developers. Once they are in, then dictate how they do, or else face service cut off. Then later label all as competitive threats then deny them services.

Points to note here are that.

The regulatory burden is excessive. It means as Facebook argued that a sale will remain open and never finalized. This is because the issues at hand arose out of the 2012 and 2014 acquisitions of Instagram and WhatsApp.

Secondly, Facebook can argue that it is simply offering its services which the people can choose to use or not because there are no other options.

I think it can only become an issue if whatever they are accused of had not been anticipated or reasonably perceived at the time. The fact that they approved all these at the time means they had also anticipated or reasonably expected Facebook to do what they are doing or accused of. Their growth to nearly 3 billion people must not alarm them and cause them to bring this lawsuit. The fact that they approve these acquisitions makes the lawsuit inappropriate unless there is significant harm to the people.

Facebook is doing what anyone in their position having their two mergers approved would do after growing to that size. This is a taught and approved method. It is not like they have done an illegal act. The law argues that there is no defense to illegality. So, we must look if Facebook has done something illegal.

TOMORROW'S WORLD ORDER'S PERSPECTIVE

We strongly believe that the accusations of anticompetitive behavior must not stand. Anyone in their position would employ the same method as taught in business school. A legal method.

A company or corporation is a legal entity with sovereign powers to determine its course of action without any interference from the government for that matter. The calls and recommendations to notify the state in its private dealings are flawed. Mind you the idea is to encourage mergers and not to be a regulatory burden and a pain. Factors to consider.

Facebook's actions or alleged misconduct and its real-world measurable harm to the consumers and competition.

Poor experiences can be harmful to consumers. Violations of privacy issues can be a harm to the consumer. Increased say advertising prices can be harmful if no cheaper alternatives are available.

Have there been consumer safety violations?

There is a relationship that exists as a result of free markets and general wealth.

Rent-Seeking as an influencing factor for the lawsuit.

Easiest to obtain and requires no skills at all. Utilization of resource ownership. Companies, especially new ones, can practice the art of rent-seeking by asking the government to provide subsidies and lower tariffs. The company can point to barriers of entry or stiffened competition that can trigger the interstates or the Federal Trade Commission to act and bring a lawsuit against the market shareholder.

The idea behind this is one of a perfect market system where there is competition. The idea of a lot of small companies is appealing. The assumption here is that the system is perfect and efficient. The development of new technologic based markets resembles perfect competition. What the interstate and the government have in mind are large numbers of sellers and buyers. There are many smaller firms instead of one large corporation. The products they sell are homogenous for example there are not many differences between advertising spaces. Supply and demand are constant due to large numbers of players. The interstates have a greater role in the provision of perfect information availability. What they do not realize is that their regulations make everything prohibitively expensive. The first wave of development is characterized by many social media networks and sites all with no market share. There is usually a fake boom. No initial cost in terms of renting costs and any capital costs.

X.

RECOMMENDATIONS AND THE WAY FORWARD.

Laws provide legal precedence that sets the benchmark so that to some extent the whole thing is predictable to a certain extent. But what do we do in changing circumstances? We must also look at the factors that influenced some of these Acts and laws. Surely factors then cannot be factors now and this calls for major reforms and changes to the legal system. The growth of current corporations has seen a new form of global power and a new form of political influence.

That calls also for a new form of global governance in Tomorrow's World Order in response to the issues we have at hand. It can no longer be justified to regulate for the sake of regulating. Gone are the days when people have this skewed fantasy about governments running the show. They had time over the past seventy years to show us the way and sadly they failed. Only corporations with the resources they have, and the powers and political influence must be left to bring wealth to all humankind to levels never imagined before. I have pointed out that the idea of a perfect market with a lot of buyers and sellers is just a fantasy and does not exist in the real world. This rollback mechanism to take people back to the starting line just because people are afraid of what these Trusts and corporations can do can no longer be justified. It is time to take a different road. The power of these corporations must not be underestimated. They can play big roles in doing what the governments cannot do at the time. They must be monitored in a facilitating manner. Guided by us as Tomorrow's World Order.

There is general hostility towards the corporations and trusts. This is understandable but let fear not stop us from getting better than we are getting now. Trusts and corporations can be good. The rule of reason can be applied but I think more must be done to reform the laws so that emphasis is not placed on anticompetitive behavior.

The long-term benefits must be given more importance than just competition. Economies of scale can help lower cost significantly in the long run. So, exercise patience. Long-term benefits must outweigh increased competition, etc.

FACILITATION RATHER THAN A REGULATORY BURDEN.

Regulatory burden means a continuous vicious cycle with no long-term benefits. That triggers the need for the rollback mechanism with its fake booms as corporations are broken up but with no long-term benefits. But a facilitating approach means the corporations will grow to become complex structures that will utilize the economies of scale to offer consumers the best quality products at lowered prices. This is the only way to raise living standards taking most of the people out of the poverty zone. Our job as Tomorrow's World Order will be to act as the overseer to make sure that they will pass the benefits to the consumers. That they will not violate their positions due to their size and power and abuse the consumers, etc. Read also Tomorrow's World Order to see our road map.

Regulatory burden increases the cost of running corporations in that in the end it will be impossible to pass over the benefits to the consumer.

Is the government or Federal Trade Commission correct to restrict a company from merging with others on competition grounds? Especially in an economic environment where they are failing to do what they are supposed to do. Like, provide cheaper accommodation which has become the job of the corporations in recent years. The global issues now and the poor living standards means the current approach is not working. These corporations in the long run have the ability and resources to lift all humanity out of the poverty zone through wages and provision of services.

TOMORROW'S WORLD ORDER'S PERSPECTIVE

Governments have become very trickery using abolished practices when they discovered a technologically advanced way of doing the same thing as in slavery. Now human-hacking everyone and using drone technology to do the same as during slavery. This has led to the shift of trust from the government to these corporations and Trusts who have kind of taken over from the government. The smaller companies have realized that threats are the government agencies rather than the big companies. This is because they tend to control what customers they get and when determining what they can get say per month in revenue that everything is controlled. The idea is to do away with obsolete institutions. Competitive and the changing environment has meant reduced tariffs collection. Reduced rent and taxes, etc. This has led them to use trickery methods like hacking people and their mobile phones to kind of control and regulate. Now the fears are from the interstate and the government bodies rather than the people themselves. All these lawsuits are a survival strategy as the big corporations have taken the small firms in their wings and are all operating as one providing software development and cloud-based computing, etc. That has left the interstate and the government bodies unable to justify development packages as the numbers seeking their services are becoming less and less.

NEED TO ACKNOWLEDGE THE INADEQUACIES OF THE CURRENT SYSTEM IN DEALING WITH THE EVER-GROWING CORPORATIONS.

The growth of these poses a real challenge. Governments are obliged to protect people's essential rights from abuse by these corporations. But the challenge is in managing these as they operate interstate and in foreign countries. The Federal was nominated to deal with these but so far, they have become frustrative and made the whole thing cumbersome and expensive. A new form of global governance is needed and only we can handle the situation. This is because the interstate and the Federal agents have made everything a personal thing. A survival tactic where it is either the corporations or them who will end out of business. This is because the growth of all these will herald the exit of all these and the arrival of new world order. We then become the referees. Now there is a conflict of interest if you like. The corporations have taken all the small companies with them living the interstate alone with reduced investment and development packages.

ABOUT DAVID GOMADZA

Founder and President of TOMORROW'S WORLD ORDER a registered global political party. Registered in Great Britain.

TOMORROW'S WORLD ORDER'S PERSPECTIVE

TOMORROW'S WORLD ORDER'S PERSPECTIVE

Antitrust Laws
The Case of Facebook v FTC

TOMORROW'S WORLD ORDER'S PERSPECTIVE